T0314819

Children and Computers in School

Children and Computers in School

Betty A. Collis
University of Twente, The Netherlands
Gerald A. Knezek
University of North Texas, USA
Kwok-Wing Lai
University of Otago, New Zealand
Keiko T. Miyashita
Tokyo Institute of Technology, Japan
Willem J. Pelgrum
Tjeerd Plomp
University of Twente, The Netherlands
Takashi Sakamoto
National Institute of Multimedia Education, Japan

Routledge
Taylor & Francis Group
New York   London

First published by
Lawrence Erlbaum Associates, Inc., Publishers
10 Industrial Avenue
Mahwah, New Jersey 07430

This edition published 2013 by Routledge
711 Third Avenue, New York, NY 10017
2 Park Square, Milton Park, Abingdon, Oxon OX14 4RN

Routledge is an imprint of the Taylor & Francis Group, an informa business

Cover design by Gail Silverman
Illustration by Justin Silverman

Library of Congress Cataloging-in-Publication Data

Children and Computers in School / Betty A. Collis ... [et al.]
     p.   cm.
     Includes indexes.
     ISBN 0-8058-2073-6 (cloth : alk. paper). — ISBN
0-8058-2074-4 (pbk. : alk. paper)
     1. Computer-assisted instruction—Cross-cultural stud-
ies.   2. Computers and children—Cross-cultural studies.
I. Collis, Betty.
LB1028.43.C45   1996
371.3'34—dc20   96-18083
                                                        CIP

Contents

Preface

This book contains findings from three multinational studies about children using computers in school. Its seven authors from four nations were key researchers on these projects.

The first chapter places children and their use of computers in school within the broader context of the information age, whereas the second provides an overview of the three studies. Chapters 3, 4, and 5 each focus in detail on findings from one of the three studies. Chapter 6 contains reflections written by individuals or pairs of authors about the implications of the findings from the book as a whole.

The final form of this book conforms quite closely to the initial plan agreed on after discussions among the authors. Nevertheless, some significant modifications have been made along the way. The most important of these is the decision to combine two conceptually related chapters on "findings" and "implications" into one chapter containing reflections on the significance of the findings by several of the authors, in separate sections. A thought-provoking essay about how culture influences and is influenced by information technology has been included as an appendix as well. This was written by M. A. Murray-Lasso, a researcher from Mexico participating in one of the three studies.

The level of detail varies greatly from chapter to chapter in this book. We have purposely confined most of the intricacies of research designs, sampling procedures, statistical techniques, and other methodological issues to chapters 3 through 5. This enables perusal of chapters 1, 2, and 6 by casual readers in order to learn the gist of our findings. Fellow scholars in the field will probably wish to examine chapters 3 through 5 in detail.

In the broadest sense, this work has been both a study of and a product of the information age. Only by extensive use of the Internet has it been possible to finish in a timely and affordable manner. Otherwise, the information to be conveyed may have been outdated by the time it reached the reader, if it all had to be compiled and routed at international postal service speeds. A case in point is that airmail delivery required more than 5 weeks to simply route the contract among all authors for signatures, whereas most electronic mail discussions on critical issues were settled within a few days.

As with any book of this nature, many people in addition to the authors contributed to the completion of the manuscript. Hollis Heimbouch, former senior editor for Lawrence Erlbaum Associates, supported the original concept of this book and maintained an unwavering belief in the authors through several modifications and delays. Savanee Bangpibob and Pijarn Chareonsri gave a unified look to the tables and figures. Rhonda Christensen, Vicki Inouye, Lois Knezek, Luz Amparo Martinez, Akira Sakamoto, Robert Scannell, and Hershel Strickland each provided helpful feedback as native and non-native English readers of various portions and editions of the manuscript.

Several of the book's authors contributed special talents to this project. Takashi Sakamoto first introduced most members of the authoring team to each other (he participated in all three multinational studies). Betty Collis was especially clear thinking during discussions about the form and content of the book, while Collis, Kwok-Wing Lai, and I were primarily responsible for formative evaluations and final checks on the accuracy and coherence of the book as a whole. Final copy was assembled at the University of North Texas, and I alone accept responsibility for any errors which may remain.

—*Gerald A. Knezek*

Chapter 1

Children in the Information Age

Betty A. Collis
Takashi Sakamoto

LIVING IN THE INFORMATION AGE

There is little doubt that far-reaching changes have occurred throughout the world within our lifetimes that make the society in which children in the 1990s are growing up different from that for which their parents, grandparents, and teachers prepared. Information and communication technologies are a central part of these changes, both as agents and as servants. The ability to access, and treat as your own, information and computing power only available a few decades ago to a relatively few, has now become part of the daily life of an increasingly greater portion of mankind. Being able to deal with and exploit information technologies (IT) and increasingly, their convergence with communication technologies, is becoming a core expectation of literacy and social functionality.

As typical examples, within a few months in 1994, in popular newspapers in countries as geographically dispersed as the United States, Canada, Brazil, The Netherlands, France, the United Kingdom, Australia, Japan, China, and Hong Kong, we have seen on an almost daily basis articles referring to the Internet, to working and learning at home via a multimedia "information highway," to new computer products such as CD-ROMs and new operating systems and new types of computer software to support group work and distributed computing. We have come to expect that we can communicate with people around the world, at our convenience, in a variety of ways. These of course include ordinary postal service, but increasingly just as likely, are the telephone, facsimile transmission (fax), electronic mail (e-mail), and now, just emerging, new forms of "telepresence" such as desktop conferencing.

In addition, we accept without need for elaboration that "the computer" has information about us and for us and presents decisions to us with which we often cannot argue. "The computer" prepares our bills and makes decisions about where we work and study and where we can have reservations for vacations or health care. We increasingly expect to go to computers or computer-facilitated mass media, rather than teachers or textbooks, for information we feel is relevant. Our computer-mediated retrieval needs range from tomorrow's weather to interpretations of world events. We have, in one or two decades, learned a new vocabulary, related to computers, that brings a universal feeling to language and reference that the world has never seen, even in the days of Latin and the Roman Empire. Although we worried as educators in the 1970s and early 1980s that we must be responsible to teach this vocabulary to our students, society has now taken most of the burden from us. Because of the computer's permeation throughout our working and entertainment worlds, some functional awareness of computer-related technology has become part of the normal experience of young and old, rich and poor, clever and disinterested, throughout the world.

A major indicator of the rapid growth of ITs is their pervasiveness in the office and factory. Computers are now commonplace desktop resources throughout the world, and e-mail is replacing fax as a standard form of business operation. A continual stream of new technological developments comes into the marketplace, many of which are becoming rapidly accepted in workplace practice. Consider the following list of ITs judged by commercial organizations in the United States as having the greatest impact on their business practices in 1994 (from Cook & Cohen, 1994, p. 47):

- computer-aided design
- paperless manufacturing
- groupware
- online services
- document management
- customer service technology
- point-of-sale terminals
- servers
- networks
- databases
- printers
- voice recognition
- storage protection
- fax machines
- scanners
- flash technology
- advanced fiber optics
- wireless technology
- videoconferencing

All of these items relate to information and communication technologies. Almost all of these are new, both in concept and in skills required for utilization, especially in comparison to what we as parents and teachers and curriculum developers are familiar with in our own experience. We have little or no expertise with many of them; we cannot provide models of good practice to our children. Thus, there are radical changes in the tools and techniques of work that have already occurred and are currently set to increase geometrically, given the new convergence of telephone, television, and computer technologies poised to enter our homes and offices.

Inexorably, more and more of us are using computers the way we use automobiles, telephones, postage stamps, pens, libraries, bookstores, calculators, and credit cards—as normal tools allowing us to live and work in increasingly abnormal ways, compared to what our parents and grandparents did. Fortunately, the standards of expertise in the information society still include fundamentals that have always been central to becoming educated. These are good communication skills, the ability to solve problems using both generalizable heuristics and local knowledge, the habit of appropriate critical thought and positive attitude, the capacity to be aware of and build on relevant prior experience, and the ability to step beyond prior experience when creativity as well as craftsmanship are valuable.

These needs have not changed in the new information age, but are being challenged and extended in ways and at a speed that the majority of people have not had to grapple with in previous times. We still must communicate well and effectively, but now, not only with those of our own culture and language, and not only with those who know us and with whom we share the expectations of communicative conduct. We still need to be problem solvers, but the local knowledge that we are to apply is increasing beyond anyone's capacity for mastery and the tools we need for dealing with problem situations are themselves a major source of new problems in themselves.

In addition, where previously we learned by modeling and respectful observation, now, ironically, we have both too much to observe and too little. There is too much in the sense that even the youngest child can see and hear and interact with a range of persons and situations so broad that historically important matters like respect, attention, sustained practice, and transfer possibilities are stretched thin almost to the point of meaninglessness. There is too little to observe in the sense that models appropriate to learn from and be measured against, for functioning effectively in the emerging information age are still not easily found, beyond the seductive models of game players, hackers, pirates, electronic criminals, or fantasylike "cybernauts."

So in this rapidly changing world, where job requirements and study require-ments and fundamental literacy expectations are changing so rapidly, what about our children? What about schools? What is happening? What should be happening? Although the essence of education—to transmit the cultural heritage to successive generations and to cultivate competencies that will enable children to adapt and construct the future society (Sakamoto, 1992)—does not change, educational content and methods do. As IT becomes part of society, it becomes part of schools and is changing their content and methods.

WHY INFORMATION TECHNOLOGY IN SCHOOLS?

Thus, inevitably, because educational content and methods change corresponding to social changes (see Sakamoto, 1992, for a discussion in the Japanese context), schools and educators have not been passive observers of the changes and challenges mentioned above. In the 1960s, researchers with access to the mainframe computers of the time began experimenting with the possibilities of using computers for learning. Tutorial software was developed and successfully used in the 1960s and 1970s in university settings in many countries, and these experiments soon came to include applications for schools. Informatics as an object of study spread from universities to secondary schools. When the arrival of microcomputers in the late 1970s brought personal computing empowerment to individuals, it also brought with it the conviction that all students must become computer literate, and that schools had the responsibility to prepare their students to realize the potential of the empowerment.

Thus, during the late 1970s and 1980s, computers became part of the school, in at least some of the schools in probably every country of the world. Many countries began broadscale policy initiatives relating to school computing access. Inventories and analyses of the initiatives can be found in many sources. For example, a good international overview can be seen in the many publications of the International Federation for Information Processing Technical Committee 3 (IFIP TC 3) over the period 1975 until the present.[1] Under the auspices of IFIP, for three decades invited specialists in computers in education from countries throughout the world have regularly developed comprehensive overviews of the field.[2] Recent examples include McDowell and McDougall (1990), Johnson and Samways (1993), and Lewis and Mendelsohn (1994).

And IFIP TC 3 is only one of many sources of analyses of trends in IT in education. In 1994, for example, there were more than 75 international scientific journals in the English language alone relating to different aspects of educational technology, generally involving computers. There are extensive local publications, books, and other resources in countries throughout the world. International agencies such as the United Nations Education, Scientific & Cultural Organization (UNESCO) and the World Bank stimulate different collections of trends and analyses.[3]

Many analyses have been done of prospective motives for nations committing resources and policy to IT. Hawkridge (1991), for example, has noted six major motivations:

---

[1] IFIP coordinates the work of various specialists groups professionally involved with computer technology. TC 3 relates to informatics and education.

[2] For a complete listing of IFIP TC3 publications as well as information about the current activities and members of its working groups, contact the international office of the IFIP Secretariat, Hofstrasse 3, A-2361 Laxenburg, Austria

[3] See, for example, the Proceedings of the First World Congress, Education and Informatics: Strengthening International Co-operation, UNESCO, 1989. A second UNESCO World Congress is under preparation for July 1996.

1. The social rationale: Computers are important in society, thus students should be prepared to deal with them.
2. The vocational rationale: Students should use computers to prepare for future jobs.
3. The pedagogical rationale: Computers can improve instruction in traditional subject areas.
4. The catalytic rationale: Computers will set off wide-ranging changes in the educational system itself and change the nature of teaching and learning.
5. The IT industry rationale: Supporting computers in schools will help build up a market for a country's internal hardware and software production capability.
6. The cost-effectiveness rationale: Computers can replace teachers or some of the costs of teachers.

Each of these motivations call for some kind of measure of success, or prediction of future success. Educational researchers, economists, policy makers, educational decision makers, teachers, parents, vendors, designers, teacher educators, learning psychologists, curriculum specialists, sociologists, philosophers, and politicians all have their own reasons and yardsticks for wanting to know about the impact of computers in schools. From hundreds of different perspectives research has been done and is being done, trying to assess this impact.

RESEARCH PERSPECTIVES ON CHILDREN AND INFORMATION TECHNOLOGY

The fact that research activity in this area continues unabated despite many years of intense activity relates to a number of factors. Clearly the field itself is continually expanding as the technology grows and offers new opportunities and learning possibilities. Multimedia and its educational applications have generated considerable research attention. The "Information Superhighway" and its current realization, the Internet, are stimulating a recurrence of possibilities in the mid-1990s parallel to those seen for computer literacy a decade earlier. For example, the director of learning technologies for the U.S. Council of Chief State School Officers made the proclamation in 1994 that:

> access to the National Information Infrastructure for education will determine the haves and have-nots of the next generation. From preschool to graduate school, learners must have access to the information highway. The challenge is universal access that is affordable for communities and individuals. Learners of all ages must be able to use the technology for everything from contact with the Library of Congress to job retraining programs in adult life. All citizens, whether they are in inner cities or remote rural areas, must use these services if our people are to remain competitive in the world marketplace. (Withrow, 1994, p. 2)

Technological advances in other forms of networked computing are stimulating new interests in cooperative work and cooperative learning (for a review, see Collis, 1994). Various theoretical frameworks for anchoring investigations of computer-use impact bring with them new surges of research activity. Examples are frameworks derived from the work of Vygotsky (1986), which considers the social environment as an integral part of the process of cognitive change, and those based on concepts of constructivism, in which learning is seen as intrinsically motivated problem solving based on personal discovery (Cooper, 1993). One can foresee the possibility of another round of research emerging from virtual reality as viewed in Vygotskyan and constructivist frameworks.

In addition, the sheer increase in the numbers of computers in schools and the amount of time and effort that has been expended on training teachers, preparing learning materials, and exploring possibilities for the technology, is starting to generate a call for accountability, for "results" and evidence of cost-effectiveness, alongside the calls for more exploration, more provision, more time, and more support. In the Netherlands, for example, after 10 years of extensive Ministry support for national initiatives relating to the development of educational software, teacher training, and hardware and software provision to schools, the Ministry policy in the mid-1990s has now become one of standing back and letting schools decide for themselves how they wish to continue with IT. The assumption is that applications of perceived worth will be chosen by the schools, that there has been enough time for preliminary exploration with computers, and that schools and teachers can now make their own decisions about how best to choose and proceed (Van Deursen & Moonen, 1991). Thus, reasons for continued research on the impact of computer use in schools remain prominent and even increase, especially as the practitioner is increasingly becoming more responsible for personal decision making about computer applications for learning support.

But parallel to the accumulation of research activity with respect to the impact of computers in education has been an accumulation of comment about the limitations and inadequacies of much of the ongoing research. Clark (1985) for example, stimulated much debate with his arguments about confounding in educational computing research, a debate that is far from settled.[4] Many have argued the interrelationship of any sort of impact of computer use on an individual learner with cultural artifacts and social processes outside the individual (see, e.g., Newman, 1990). The need for broad, naturalist perspectives, for comparative analysis transcending the boundaries of the circumstances and interpretation of the individual researcher, is one response to these limitations and interrelationships.

However, wide-scale, multicultural, multivariable research studies are complex activities requiring infrastructure, opportunity, and a mix of initiatives, circumstances, and financial support beyond the possibilities of the majority of those interested in the impact of IT in education, and in particular on children. Thus, relatively few research studies (as compared to inventories or compilations of

---

[4]See, for example, the special issue of the journal *Educational Technology Research and Development* (Ross, 1994).

trends) have been carried out that systematically involve large numbers of coun-tries, cultures, subjects, comparative situations, and common measurement proce-dures. If the impact of IT on children is to be understood in a generalizable way, then such wide-scale studies are invaluable, not only to document the impacts that seem to transcend local variabilities, but also to document what impacts are inextricably culture and context sensitive. And not only should such studies involve the characteristics of multiculturalism and standardized observation; they should also bring a variety of perspectives into focus. At the very least, the school as an organization, the classroom, the teacher, the content and methods of instruction, and the skills, insights and attitudes of the children themselves all must receive attention.

One particular issue is the nature of the impact on the child himself. Given the many possibilities for IT in society and education, it is natural that its impact on something more than production variables, such as time to learn particular skills, should also be an object of research. Variables relating to growth in higher level cognitive functioning, such as increased habits of self-reflection and self-evaluation, increased consideration of alternatives in a problem situations, more effective planning, and more positive attitudes about learning and one's self as a problem solver, are also important to study in a cross-cultural perspective.

WHY THIS BOOK?

Fortunately, these characteristics and perspectives have been brought together in three large-scale, long-term international research projects, all relating to the impact of computer use in education on children. These three projects are the focus of this book, and are introduced in chapter 2 before they are discussed in detail in chapters 3, 4, and 5, and synthesized and reflected on as a set in chapter 6. Each of these research projects—CompEd, ITEC, and YCCI—has its own particular history and context but there is interlinkage among them, to a certain extent because some of the key researchers involved were associated with more than one of the projects, but more fundamentally because each supplies a particular focus or insight that complements the others.

CompEd takes the broadest view, looking at schools as organizations through the impressions of their principals, their computer coordinators, and their teachers, and through overviews of student activities and functional competencies with IT. ITEC focuses on the classroom and studies in more depth the interactions of teachers, students, and computers in classroom settings. YCCI continues the focusing in process, moving into the impressions and thoughts of children them-selves relative to IT and its impact on them. Although each of these research projects has itself generated a wide range of literature, the opportunity has not yet occurred for the three projects to be brought into synergy with each other—until this book.

Thus, even as IT is having immeasurable impact on society as a whole, it is also having an impact on education, on its content and methods. But how is it affecting children themselves? Through the three international studies analyzed in this book we will be in a stronger position to give a response to this question.

REFERENCES

Clark, R. E. (1985). Confounding in educational computing research. *Journal of Educational Computing Research, 1*(2), 137–148.

Collis, B. A. (1994). Collaborative learning and CSCW: Research perspectives for internetworked educational environments. In R. Lewis & P. Mendelsohn (Eds.), *Lessons from learning* (pp. 81–101). Amsterdam: North Holland.

Cook, W. J., & Cohen, W. (1994, May 2). 25 breakthroughs that are changing the way we live and work. *U.S. News and World Report*, 46–60.

Cooper, P. A. (1993). Paradigm shifts in designed instruction: From behaviorism to cognitivism to constructivism. *Educational Technology, 33*(5), 12–19.

Hawkridge, D. (1991). Machine-mediated learning in third-world schools? *Machine-Mediated Learning, 3*, 319–328.

Johnson, D. C., & Samways, B. (Eds.). (1993). *Informatics and changes in learning*. Amsterdam: North-Holland/Elsevier.

Lewis, R., & Mendelsohn, P. (Eds.). (1994). *Lessons from learning*. Amsterdam: North Holland/Elsevier.

McDowell, A., & McDougall, C. (Eds.). (1990). *Computers in education*. Amsterdam: North Holland/Elsevier.

Newman, D. (1990). Opportunities for research on the organizational impact of school computers. *Educational Researcher, 19*(3), 8–13.

Ross, S. M. (Ed.). (1994). Media and Methods. *Educational Technology Research and Development, 42* (2, Special issue) .

Sakamoto, T. (1992). Impact of informatics on school education systems: National strategies for the introduction of informatics into schools. *Education & Computing, 8*, 129–135.

UNESCO. (1989). *Education and informatics: Strengthening international co-operation*. Paris: Author.

Van Deursen, J. I., & Moonen, J. (1991). *Een actieve school met elektronische leermiddelen* [An active school with electronic learning material] (OPSTAP-reeks 27). Zoetermeer, Netherlands: Ministry of Education and Science.

Vygotsky, L. S. (1986). *Thought and language*. Cambridge, MA: MIT Press.

Withrow, F. (1994). New organization formed to coordinate national education and training technology. *The ISTE Update Newsletter, 6*(7), 1–2.

Chapter 2

Three Multinational Studies

Betty A. Collis
Gerald A. Knezek
Kwok-Wing Lai
Keiko T. Miyashita
Willem J. Pelgrum
Tjeerd Plomp
Takashi Sakamoto

In chapter 1, Collis and Sakamoto explored characteristics of information technology (IT) societies and examined several common rationales for using computers in schools. In chapter 2, we introduce studies that have gathered evidence from many cultures about the effects of IT on students' cognitive and affective development. Two major themes are also introduced in chapter 2: How does one best come to understand the complex phenomenon of children interacting with IT? What "results" or findings are emerging across cultures and settings? This chapter sets the stage for the findings and their implications presented later in the book.

VIEWS ACROSS MANY CULTURES

Three multinational studies form the foundation of this book: the International Association for the Evaluation of Educational Achievement Computers in Education Project (IEA CompEd), the Information Technology in Education and Children Project (ITEC), and the Young Children's Computer Inventory Project (YCCI). Taken together, these projects span elementary, middle school (lower secondary), and secondary education. Their findings about the psychological impact of school computer use are based on data gathered in 19, 16, and 3 nations, respectively.

The studies present three complimentary views of the effects of computer use in school environments. IEA is at the most global level, looking at school systems, with their many different aspects—policy, practice, teachers, and principals. ITEC is at the next, more focused level—selected classrooms form the research units, with a more detailed study of the "ecosystems" that include children and IT. YCCI looks most specifically at the children themselves and how IT might be affecting their ways of thinking about themselves. An overview of each of the studies is provided in the sections that follow.

IEA COMPED

This international comparative survey of computers in education (CompEd) ran from 1987 until 1994. It was conducted under the auspices of the International Association for the Evaluation of Educational Achievement (IEA).

The IEA

The IEA is a nongovernmental international organization of professional educational research centers from more than 50 national educational systems (Hayes, 1993). The organization has been in existence for more than 30 years. IEA researchers undertake international comparative research projects in core school subjects like mathematics, science, and native language mastery (mother tongue).

The history of IEA dates back to late 1958, when representatives from approximately 12 countries concluded at a UNESCO meeting in Hamburg that there was a strong need to conduct empirically oriented international comparative research in order to study problems common to many educational systems. The first feasibility study (conducted in 12 countries for a population of 13-year-old students) involved testing in reading comprehension, mathematics, science, geography and nonverbal ability. It proved to be successful (Foshay, 1962).

Since 1962, a large number of studies have been carried out. The First Mathematics Study was conducted in 1964 in 12 countries on national probability samples of 13-year-old and preuniversity students (Husen, 1967). The Six-Subject study was administered in 1970 in 21 countries and included the following subjects: science, reading comprehension, literature, French as foreign language, English as foreign language, and civic education (Carroll, 1975; Comber & Keeves, 1973; Lewis & Massad, 1975; Purves, 1973; Thorndike, 1973; Torney, Oppenheim, & Farnen, 1976). This study identified the following three populations of students: students ages 10 and 14 and students in the final year of full-time secondary education. Twenty countries participated in the Second International Mathematics Study, for which data were collected in 1981 (Robitaille & Garden, 1989; Travers & Westbury, 1989). Other studies in the 1980s were the Second International Science Study, Written Composition, and the Preprimary Study. Increasing numbers of countries participated in more recent studies: 32 in the Reading Literacy Study (Elley, 1992) and more than 40 in the Third International Mathematics and Science Study scheduled for completion in 1997.

In general, the design of IEA studies involves collecting data at different levels of the school system (country, school, teacher and student), taking national representative samples typically from three populations of students: (a) students near the end of primary education, (b) students in the first stage of secondary education, and (c) students in the second stage of secondary education. As can be learned from IEA reports, the publications are aimed at various audiences; the general goal is to promote the understanding of the functioning of education in order to contribute to its improvement (Husen & Postlethwaite, 1985; Passow, Noah, Eckstein, & Mallea, 1976). In this way, IEA studies serve two purposes: (a) to provide policymakers and educational practitioners with information about the quality of their educational systems in relation to relevant reference groups in similar nations, and (b) to assist researchers and policymakers in understanding the reasons for observed differences among educational systems.

The CompEd Study

The IEA CompEd was conceived as a two-stage investigation. The first stage (1987–1990) was aimed at describing the worldwide situation with regard to computer use in terms of many variables. Items measured included how computers were used, the extent and availability of computers in schools, the nature of instruction about computers, and estimates of the effects that computers are having on students, the curriculum, and the school as an institution (Pelgrum & Plomp, 1991, 1993). Data were collected in the participating educational systems from a representative sample of schools and teachers at the primary, lower secondary and upper secondary levels in the participating countries. Computer education teachers, and computer-using as well as nonusing teachers in mathematics, science, and mother tongue were asked about the current state of computers in education. Quite extensive analyses were also conducted in order to explore causal linkages between the different variables.

Data collection for Stage 2 of the CompEd study commenced in 1992, after 2 years of preparation. This stage consisted of two parts, the first of which was a repetition of the survey conducted in Stage 1. Data were gathered through questionnaires distributed to principals, computer resource coordinators, and teachers, with the form and content of the questionnaires closely related to those used in Stage 1. In this way, it was possible to determine the rate of development of computers in education over time.

The second purpose of Stage 2 was to study variables at the student level. Issues addressed included the extent to which students had access to computers, ways in which computers were used in schools and outside schools, the extent of student IT competencies, and student attitudes toward and perceptions of computers. Students were surveyed at three age/grade levels:

Population 1: students in the grade in which the modal age is 10 years.
Population 2: students in the grade in which the modal age is 13 years.

Population 3: students in the penultimate (next-to-last) year of secondary education.

Participating Educational Systems

Because some countries operate more than one educational system, IEA prefers to use the word *system* instead of country. Table 2.1 lists the systems that were participating in the CompEd Study.

TABLE 2.1
Overview of Project Characteristics: IEA-CompEd

	Years of Data Collection	
	1989	1992
Participating countries	Austria, Belgium-Flemish, Belgium-French, Canada-BC, China, France, Germany, Greece, Hungary, India, Israel, Italy, Japan, Luxembourg, Netherlands, New Zealand, Poland, Portugal, Slovenia, Switzerland, U.S.	Austria, Bulgaria, Germany, Greece, India, Israel, Japan, Latvia, Netherlands, Slovenia, Thailand, U.S.
School types	Elementary education Lower secondary education Upper secondary education	Elementary education Lower secondary education Upper secondary education
Respondents	School principals Computer coordinators Computer education teachers Teachers of mathematics Teachers of science Teachers of mother tongue	School principals Computer coordinators Teachers of professional computer education students
Research type	Survey	Survey
Instruments	Questionnaires	Questionnaires Multiple–choice tests Performance tests
Samples	National representative	National representative
Supported by	International Association for the Evaluation of Educational Achievement	International Association for the Evaluation of Educational Achievement

Snapshot of Major Findings

Some of the major conclusions from the survey in 1989 were:

- There were large differences between countries in access to computers.
- There was not enough hardware or software.
- Teachers were insufficiently trained.
- Extent of integration of instructional tool software was strongly related to availability.

Some major findings from the 1992 survey were:

- A greater number of schools were equipped with computers than in 1989.
- More hardware was available in schools.
- Hardware quality was improving, but slowly.
- There was more instructional software available.
- There was somewhat more integration, but not in all countries.
- There were fewer complaints about hardware/software shortages among educational practitioners.
- Not all students used computers.
- There were large differences within and among countries in computer-related knowledge among students.
- Students learn much about computers outside school.
- Boys knew more about computers than girls.
- Boys liked working with computers more than girls.

These and other findings are discussed in detail in chapter 3.

ITEC

ITEC stands for Information Technology in Education and Children and is the name of a long-term international research project associated with UNESCO and many other organizations. Phase I began in 1988 and was completed in 1992. It involved over its 4-year span more than 30 researchers in 25 countries. A brief overview of the ITEC Project is provided in Table 2.2.

Purpose

The central research question of ITEC can be stated succinctly:

In the context of various combinations of background variables,under what combinations of

- characteristics of computer use,
- social interaction surrounding computer use, and

- instructional integration of computer use

is a positive impact on children's higher level cognitive functioning more likely to occur?

How do these sets of conditions vary in different cultures and countries?

TABLE 2.2
Overview of Project Characteristics: ITEC

	Years of Data Collection
	1987–1992
Participating countries (through full term of the project)	Bulgaria Canada China Costa Rica France Hungary Israel Japan Mexico Netherlands New Zealand Romania Sweden U.S. (then) U.S.S.R. Zimbabwe
School type	Elementary education (ages 9–10)
Participants (throughout the project)	26 researchers, 18 school principals, 24 teachers, 660-680 children
Research type	Multiple case study, with mixed qualitative/quantitative methods.
Instruments and procedures	Observations of classrooms, interviews, questionnaires, analysis of videotapes of classrooms, and of children in more than 40 lessons involving intensive computer activities, inventories, and other aspects of case-study development and analysis.
Sampling	Teachers nominated as having a reputation in their countries as doing "good things with computers" in classroom lessons with 9-year-old children.
Supported by	UNESCO and various national research agencies in participating countries.

Preliminary questions were also developed for the first phase of the study:

- In the context of children using computers in the classroom, what are measurable or at least observable indicators of presumed "higher level cognitive functioning"?
- Do these indicators vary cross-culturally?
- If the cross-cultural variation in the indicators of "higher level cognitive functioning" is not too great, can a reliable methodology, usable in countries around the world, be found to measure the appearance and change of these indicators over time and in the complex context of the computer-use setting?

The 32 experts from 14 nations participating in the planning meeting held in Bulgaria, in May 1988, concluded that these kinds of questions were important to pursue:

The ITEC Project has the potential to make a strong contribution to both research and practice in the application of IT in education. The application is occurring world-wide despite the lack of a synthesized base of information about its impact on child development or on the system of culturally sensitive variables surrounding the child in his experiences with IT in education. We have the opportunity to make a significant contribution, on behalf of the child, to the eventual recommendation of uses of IT in education most likely to be of positive impact to him and his development. (Collis, 1993, p. 7)

Method

The ITEC research was based on classrooms as research unit *ecosystems*, using Vygotskian theoretical foundations and mixed qualitative–quantitative research methods. It was decided to seek out existing classrooms in participating countries where teachers of students ages 9 to 10 were known to be doing "good things" in terms of computer-use instructional settings. Interviews were administered to principals at participating schools, and researchers in the participating countries completed observation checklists and interviews within 23 selected classrooms from 16 countries where computer use was already established with 9- and 10-year-old children and where the teachers had a reputation of working successfully with computers in their classrooms. Videotape footage was taken at many sites for later analysis by a team of researchers. This decision was made in order to maximize the chance of finding measurable effects on higher level cognitive functioning. At the close of observations in Fall 1990, 23 classrooms were involved in the study: one each from Bulgaria, Canada, China, Hungary, Israel, Japan, the Netherlands, New Zealand, Sweden, the United States, Russia, and Zimbabwe; two each from Costa Rica, France, and Romania; and four from Mexico. Thus, 16 countries were represented by approximately 680 students.

Analysis and Findings

In October 1990 most of the ITEC researchers were able to meet in Canada to examine the data and reach a consensus on ITEC findings. After viewing the videotapes of IT classroom activities and reviewing translated teachers' comments, the researchers categorized behaviors seen during computer-using student activities into the following 10 classes of evidence of metacognitive development:

1. Relating a problem to previous problems
2. Formulating appropriate questions
3. Trying alternative approaches
4. Evaluating one's actions
5. Analyzing problems
6. Recognizing relationships
7. Generating new ideas
8. Synthesizing information
9. Observing central issues and problems
10. Comparing similarities and differences (Collis, 1993).

These condensed categories were then used by the researchers to judge how many of the indicators they had observed in the classes that they had visited and videotaped. It was then possible to include researcher as well as teacher judgments when drawing conclusions from the data.

Some of the major findings of ITEC Phase 1 related to student metacognition were:

• 91% of the participating teachers reported observing one or more indicators of higher level cognitive skills among their IT-using students.
• The majority of the researcher-observers also reported one or more students displaying higher level thinking behaviors during the IT-using class.
• The student metacognitive skills most frequently observed by researchers were: (a) analyzing problems, (b) evaluating one's actions, and (c) formulating appropriate questions.
• Teachers and researchers reported that the students in IT classrooms developed new strategies for working with peers, were very motivated, and enjoyed and became more self-confident in their work (Collis, 1993, p. 252).

These behaviors associated with higher order cognitive activity occurred, regardless of type of computer use, of type or number of computers, type of instructional activity, or cultural context. The common factors were enthusiastic and good teachers, supported by principals convinced that computer-use was valuable for young children.

The findings from ITEC Phase 1 are discussed in detail in chapter 4.

YCCI

The Young Children's Computer Inventory Project (YCCI) was begun in 1990 as a longitudinal study of childhood computing in school. The project was designed to provide findings from students in Grades 1 to 3 to complement two other multinational studies (ITEC and IEA CompEd) addressing the effects of IT on students at higher grade levels (Collis & Jablensky, 1989; Pelgrum & Plomp, 1991). The project was conceptualized primarily as a quantitative policy study rather than a test of a psychological theory.

Project Rationale

The YCCI Project began as a Japan–U.S. collaborative effort to search for three kinds of evidence related to the use of computers in primary schools:

1. Evidence that early computer exposure in school can have a positive, lasting impact on children's attitudes toward computers.
2. Evidence that computers can have a positive, lasting effect on learning-related dispositions such as creative tendencies, motivation, and study habits.
3. Evidence that computer use by primary school students does not have significant negative side effects such as loss of touch with reality or diminished concern for the welfare of fellow human beings.

With respect to the first goal, previous studies had indicated that computer access can improve attitudes toward computers for students of high school and college ages (D'Souza, 1988; Justen, Adams, & Waldrop, 1988). A Soviet–U.S. study of 8- to 12-year-old children also supported this claim (Martin, Heller, & Mahmoud, 1992). However, no previous studies were known to have documented this effect for children as young as Grade 1 in school. The second goal was strongly emphasized in the United States. There teachers supported the early introduction of computers (Bruder, 1990) and previous research provided encouraging results (Clements 1987; Clements & Nastasi, 1988; Lehrer & Randle 1987; Lever, Sherrod, & Bransford, 1989), but pressure continued to mount to document the educational effectiveness of computers in school. The third goal was emphasized more strongly in Japan. There computers were purposely not introduced into public elementary schools during most of the 1980s (Knezek, Miyashita, & Sakamoto, 1990), while both the "light and dark sides" of increased computer exposure were being contemplated (National Council on Educational Reform, 1986, 1987).

The initial research plan was to compare quantitative data on attitudes among students at schools newly equipped with computers in Japan, with attitudes at comparable Japanese schools not possessing computers, using time-synchronized data from the United States as a cross-cultural control. Mexico was added as a new research initiative for 1992 in order to provide a third cultural perspective. An overview of the YCCI project is provided in Table 2.3.

TABLE 2.3
Overview of Project Characteristics: YCCI

	Years of Data Collection
	1990–1993
Participating countries	Japan Mexico (1991–1992) United States
School type	Primary education Grades 1–4 (ages 6–10)
Participants	7 schools in Japan 2 Japanese Advancement Schools in U.S. 2 schools in Mexico 5 bilingual Hispanic schools in U.S. 10 English-language schools in U.S.
Research type	Quantitative, pseudoexperimental, pretest–posttest Longtitudinal trend analysis Qualitative enhancements
Instruments and procedures	Likert-type student self-report questionnaires Observations of labs and classrooms Interviews with teachers and administrators
Sampling	Urban, suburban, rural schools with and without computers paired in Japan; schools with computers selected for same categories plus public vs. private in U.S.; Spanish-speaking schools selected for geographic dispersion in Mexico and U.S.
Supported by	Fulbright Foundation Japan Society for the Promotion of Science Meadows Foundation Texas Center for Education Technology

Instrumentation

The YCCI instrument was developed to carry out project research (Miyashita & Knezek, 1992). It is a 48-item Likert-type self-rating questionnaire measuring six psychological dispositions (prevailing attitudes): Computer Importance, Computer Enjoyment, Motivation/Persistence, Study Habits, Empathy, and Creative Tendencies (Knezek & Miyashita, 1993). With respect to overall project goals, Computer Importance and Computer Enjoyment served as measurement indicators for Goal 1, whereas Motivation/Persistence, Study Habits, and Creative Tendencies served as measurement indicators for Goal 2. Empathy was the measurement indicator for Goal 3.

Subjects

Student responses from 46 school administrations were included in the study (Knezek, Miyashita, & Sakamoto, 1994). Schools from Japan and the United States were included in questionnaire administrations for each of the years 1990, 1991, 1992, and 1993. Data from Mexico schools were also included in 1992. The pilot test year was 1990, with data collected from Grades 1 and 2 at three schools. In 1991, data were also collected from students in Grades 1 and 2, but at 14 sites. In 1992, data were collected from Grades 1 through 3 at 21 school sites, and, in 1993, from Grades 1 through 4 at 8 school sites. Some subjects at selected schools provided data three consecutive years, as they advanced through three grade levels.

Selected Findings

Some of the major conclusions drawn from the study were as follows:

- Computer use in primary school has a strong positive impact on attitudes toward computers.
- Educationally relevant computer activities can have a positive impact on motivation and study habits, over the course of several years.
- Gender differences with respect to attitudes toward computers do not generally exist at the first-grade level; they probably do not emerge until after Grade 3.
- Evidence indicates that creative children may choose to use computers, rather than computer use fostering creative tendencies.
- Student perceptions of computers and school are surprisingly similar for children residing in their native cultures in Japan, Mexico, and the United States.
- Japanese students whose families are temporarily (for a few years) residing in the United States maintain dispositions very similar to their peers in Japan.
- Bilingual Hispanic immigrants to the United States appear to commonly possess and maintain learning-related dispositions more positive than either their Spanish-speaking counterparts in Mexico or their English-speaking peers in the United States.

Nineteen major findings are presented in chapter 5.

WAYS OF KNOWING

The studies described in this chapter used several different techniques to determine the effect of computer use on children in school. The IEA study initially focused on the frequency and ways in which computers were used, and the achievement-related outcomes of the introduction of IT. IEA sought to describe the impact of computer use on the "system" of education. The ITEC study, on the other hand, chose to observe students using computers in their normal classroom learning environments, and rely on the expert judgments of researchers, principals, and teachers to determine the impact. The focus was on the effect of computer use on student's higher cognitive functions. The YCCI Project asked the students to supply their own perceptions of how computer use was affecting their psychological dispositions. In some cases, the same students were asked to rate themselves for 3 or 4 consecutive years. These complementary methods become especially significant when findings from one method reconfirm the results derived through another. Cross-verification greatly increases confidence in the accuracy of the results.

One characteristic common to all three studies was their reliance on cross-cultural data, or, more accurately, their use of transnational data from many cultures. IEA gathered data from 21 educational systems in 19 nations, whereas ITEC looked at 23 classroom ecosystems in 16 countries. YCCI studied students in their indigenous cultures for 3 nations, plus a "between cultures" Japanese-living-in-America group of students, and a "first-generation-immigrant-culture" of bilingual Hispanic students residing in the United States. All studies had the potential of meeting the criterion that findings can be considered "robust" if they are supported in at least three cultures (Foschi, 1980). That is, if findings are replicated in at least three cultures, then there is a sound basis for expecting that similar effects will also be found in other cultures .

The next three chapters examine each study's cross-cultural findings. These form the foundation for the synthesis of findings and the generalized implications presented in chapter 6.

REFERENCES

Bruder, I. (1990). School interest grows as televised classroom news battles heat up. *Electronic Learning*, 9(4), 10–13.

Carroll, J. B. (1975). *The teaching of French as a foreign language in eight countries*. Stockholm: Almqvist & Wiksell/New York: Wiley.

Clements, D. H. (1987). Longitudinal study of the effects of Logo programming on cognitive abilities and achievement. *Journal of Educational Computing Research*, 3, 73–94.

Clements, D. H., & Nastasi, B. K. (1988). Social cognitive interactions in educational computer environments. *American Educational Research Journal*, 25, 87–106.

Collis, B. A. (Ed.). (1993). *The ITEC PROJECT: Information Technology in Education and Children* (Final Report of Phase 1; ED/93/WS/17). Paris: UNESCO, Division of Higher Education.

Collis, B. A., & Jablensky, A. (1989, April). *The ITEC Project: An international longitudinal study of the impact of information technology in education on children's cognitive development*. Paper presented at the UNESCO World Congress Education and Informatics, Paris.

Comber, L. C., & Keeves, J. P. (1973). *Science education in nineteen countries: An empirical study*. Stockholm: Almqvist &Wiksell/New York: Wiley.

D'Souza, P. V. (1988). A CAI approach to teaching an office technology course. *Journal of Educational Technology Systems*, 17(2), 135–140.

Elley, W. B. (1992). *How in the world do students read?* Hamburg: IEA.

Foschi, M. (1980). Theory, experimentation, and cross-cultural comparisons in social psychology. *Canadian Journal of Sociology*, 5, 91–102.

Foshay, A.W. (Ed.). (1962). *Educational achievement of 13-year olds in twelve countries*. Hamburg: UNESCO Institute for Education.

Hayes, W. A. (1993). *Activities, institutions, and people: IEA–guidebook 1993–1994*. The Hague: IEA.

Husen, T. (Ed.). (1967). *International study of achievement in mathematics: A comparison of twelve countries* (Vol. I and II). Stockholm: Almqvist &Wiksell/New York: Wiley.

Husen, T., & Postlethwaite, T. N. (Eds.). (1985). *The international encyclopedia of education*. Oxford, UK: Pergamon Press.

Justen, J. E., III, Adams, T. M., II, & Waldrop, P. B. (1988). Effects of small group versus individual computer-assisted instruction on student achievement. *Educational Technology*, 50–52.

Knezek, G., & Miyashita, K. (1993). *Handbook for the young children's computer inventory* Denton: Texas Center for Educational Technology.

Knezek, G., Miyashita, K., & Sakamoto, T. (1990). Computers in education: Japan vs. the United States. In A. McDowell & C. McDougal (Eds.), *Computers in education* (pp. 775–780). North-Holland: Elsevier Science Publishers B.V.

Knezek, G. A., Miyashita, K. T., & Sakamoto, T. (1994). *Young children's computer inventory final report*. Denton: Texas Center for Educational Technology.

Lehrer, R., & Randle, L. (1987). Problem solving, metacognition and composition: The effects of interactive software for first-grade children. *Journal of Educational Computing Research*, 3, 409–427.

Lever, S., Sherrod, K. B., & Bransford, J. (1989). The effects of Logo instruction on elementary students' attitudes toward computers and school. *Computers in Schools*, 6(1/2), 45–59.

Lewis, E. G., & Massad, C. E. (1975). *The teaching of english as a foreign language in ten countries*. Stockholm: Almqvist & Wiksell/New York: Wiley.

Martin, D., Heller, R., & Mahmoud, E. (1992). American and Soviet children's attitudes toward computers. *Journal of Educational Computing Research*, 8(2), 155–185.

Miyashita, K., & Knezek, G. (1992). The Young Children's Computer Inventory: A likert scale for assessing attitudes related to computers in instruction. *Journal of Computing in Childhood Education*, 3, 63–72.

National Council on Educational Reform. (1986, April 23). *Summary of second report on educational reform*. Tokyo: Government of Japan.

National Council on Educational Reform. (1987, April 1). *Third report on educational reform*. Tokyo: Government of Japan.

Passow, A. H., Noah, H. J., Eckstein, M. A., Mallea, J. R. (1976). *The national case study: An empirical comparative study of twenty-one educational systems*. Stockholm: Almqvist & Wiksell/New York: Wiley.

Pelgrum, W. J., & Plomp, Tj. (1991). *The use of computers in education worldwide: Results from the IEA Computers in Education survey in 19 education systems*. Oxford, UK: Pergamon Press.

Pelgrum, W. J., & Plomp, Tj. (1993). *The IEA study of computers in education: Implementation of an innovation in 21 education systems*. Oxford, UK: Pergamon Press.

Purves, A. C. (1973). *Literature education in ten countries: An empirical study*. Stockholm: Almqvist & Wiksell/New York: Wiley.

Robitaille, D. F., &Garden, R. A. (1989). *The IEA study of mathematics II: Contexts and outcomes of school mathematics*. Oxford, UK: Pergamon Press.

Thorndike, R. L. (1973). *Reading comprehension education in fifteen countries: An empirical study* Stockholm: Almqvist & Wiksell/New York: Wiley.

Torney, J. V., Oppenheim, A. N., & Farner, R. F. (1976). *Civic education in ten countries: An empirical study*. Stockholm: Almqvist & Wiksell/New York: Wiley.

Travers, K. J., & Westbury, I. (1989). *The IEA study of mathematics I: International analysis of mathematics curricula*. Oxford, UK: Pergamon Press.

Chapter 3

Information Technology and Children
From a Global Perspective

Willem J. Pelgrum
Tjeerd Plomp

This chapter provides a more detailed description of the methodology and findings from the International Association for the Evaluation of Educational Achievement Computers in Education Project (IEA CompEd) that was introduced in chapter 2. In addition, in the latter portion of the chapter, discussion is devoted to the implications that can be drawn from these and related results. Major findings for Phase 1 and Phase 2 surveys completed in 1989 and 1992, respectively, are listed in the results section. The discussion section includes higher order trends that span both phases of the study.

IEA COMPED RESEARCH DESIGN

The IEA CompEd Project employed survey research methods (Alreck & Settle, 1985) to gather "snapshot" data about the status of various systemwide parameters (how computers were used, the extent and availability of computers in schools, the nature of instruction about computers, and estimates of the effects that computers are having on students, the curriculum, and the school as an institution, etc.) as well as extent of knowledge about computing and attitudes held by students toward computers. Two related surveys were carried out, the first in 1989 at the school and teacher level, and the second, in 1992, at the school, teacher, and student level.

IEA POPULATION AND SAMPLE DESCRIPTION

In chapter 2 it was pointed out that student populations at the three major education levels of elementary, lower secondary (junior high), and upper secondary (high school) were used in the IEA CompEd Project. However, the populations selected for this book are the elementary and lower secondary groups. Population 1 was defined to be the class of students in which the modal age was 10 years (Grade 5). Population 2 was defined to be students in the grade in which the modal age was 13 years (Grade 8).

Population Selection

Due to the global goals of Stage 1, namely to provide a description of the status of computer use at the school level, it was decided that the data collection in Stage 1 should be aimed at grade ranges that contained the Stage 2 target population grade levels, and the target population grade levels plus or minus 1 year. This was true for all except the upper secondary education population, where Stage 1 data collection involved the target population grade level and the target population grade level minus 1 year. This criterion was applied to the administration of school-level questionnaires and computer education teacher questionnaires for Stage 1.

The following definitions were used for determining respondent categories in the IEA CompEd study:

1. Population 1 (elementary schools)
   - computer-using schools: all schools in which computers were used for teaching/learning purposes in grades in which the modal age of students was 9, 10, or 11 years (target year minus 1, target year, and target year plus 1).
   - noncomputer-using schools: all schools that did not use computers for teaching/learning purposes in grades in which the modal age of students was 9, 10, or 11 years.
   - computer-using teachers: all teachers in computer-using schools who used computers or taught about computers in the grades in which the modal age of students was respectively, 9, 10, and 11.
   - noncomputer-using teachers: all teachers in computer-using schools who did not use computers and did not teach about computers, but were teachers of grades in which the modal age of students was, respectively, 9, 10, and 11.
2. Population 2 (lower secondary schools)
   - computer-using schools: all schools in which computers were used for teaching/learning purposes in the grades in which the modal age of students was 12, 13, or 14 years.
   - noncomputer-using schools: all schools that did not use computers for teaching/learning purposes in the grades in which the modal age of students was 12, 13, or 14 years.

• computer-using teachers of existing subjects: all mathematics, science, and mother-tongue teachers in computer-using schools who provided lessons in these subjects in which computers were used in grades in which the modal age of students was 13 years.

• noncomputer-using teachers of existing subjects: all mathematics, science, and mother-tongue teachers in computer-using schools who provided lessons in these subjects, without using computers, in grades in which the modal age of students was 13 years.

• teachers of computer education: all teachers in computer-using schools who taught about computers in grades in which the modal age of students was 12, 13, and 14, respectively.

Sampling Procedures

The sampling design for this study, as developed by the International Coordinating Centre (ICC), can be summarized as follows: The population of interest was stratified according to dimensions relevant for each participating educational system (and laid down in national sampling plans to be approved by the project's sampling referee). Minimum sample sizes for using and nonusing schools (if appropriate) were specified. Schools were selected with probabilities of selection proportional to the size of the school.[1] The selected schools were asked to provide lists of names of the target groups of teachers and students based on the criteria defined earlier. Next, National Centers selected teachers and students according to specifications provided in a sampling manual.

For some countries it appeared to be necessary to deviate from this plan for technical and/or practical reasons. For instance, sometimes equal probabilities of selection were used, as it was not possible in some countries to sample schools with probabilities of selection proportional to the size of the school. Such deviations were negotiated with and approved by the ICC (after consultation with the sampling referee) before they could be incorporated in a national sampling plan. Pelgrum and Plomp (1993a) provided further details about characteristics of the realized samples for each educational system for Stage 1 of the study. Similar details for Stage 2 are included in Pelgrum, Janssen Reinen, and Plomp (1993). For the countries reported in this book, the samples at the elementary and lower secondary levels were judged to adequately represent the entire educational system. Table 3.1 shows the number of cases in each category of respondents for the countries reported in this book.

INSTRUMENTATION

Questionnaires

The CompEd measurement instruments consisted of standardized questionnaires accompanied by translation and administration manuals. These were developed and

---

[1]Oversampling of certain categories of schools was allowed.

TABLE 3.1

CompEd Cases Per Educational System and Category of Respondents

	Japan	Netherlands	United States
Elementary Level			
Schools			
using	135	239	209
nonusing	62	38	0
undetermined	0	0	0
Principals			
using	123	207	204
nonusing	66	43	3
undetermined	3	5	0
Coordinators			
using	95	208	156
nonusing	20	21	7
undetermined	7	15	44
Teachers			
using	79	94	0
undetermined	0	3	0
Opportunity to learn			
using school	0	142	186
non-using school	0	14	0
Students			
no computer use	1,799	420	25
use only outside	1,593	1,048	303
use only at school	1,218	390	470
at school and outside	1,492	1,763	3,528
Target grade	5	5	5
Mean age at test date	11.5	11.3	11.2

(continued on next page)

pilot-tested by the study's participants in close collaboration with the ICC. For each country, data about national context and policies were collected with a national questionnaire. This questionnaire addressed issues such as budgetary allocations, hardware availability, software availability and evaluation, and teacher training.

Two questionnaires were used for the collection of data at the school level about the availability of computers, school policies, and implementation of computers in schools. One questionnaire was for school principals and one was for the computer coordinator or another person who was acquainted with technical details of the available equipment and software.

	Japan	Netherlands	United States
Lower Secondary Level			
Schools			
using	165	420	196
nonusing	26	1	0
undetermined	0	0	0
Principals			
using	151	336	193
nonusing	30	2	0
undetermined	3	5	1
Coordinators			
using	137	366	137
nonusing	23	0	7
undetermined	5	5	48
Computer Teachers			
using	87	232	0
nonusing	3	0	0
undetermined	1	0	0
Opportunity to learn			
using schools	161	211	2
nonusing schools	23	1	0
Students			
no computer use	2,197	296	108
use only outside	1,205	904	86
use only at school	1,810	789	750
at school and outside	1,451	2,922	2,809
Target grade	8	8	8
Mean age at test date	14.5	14.4	14.2

Output measures of student skills regarding computers were collected by multiple-choice paper-and-pencil tests as well as performance tasks (in the case of word processing). These measures spanned the areas of functional knowledge, generic programming skills, and practical skills. Item content for the paper-and-pencil instrument, the Functional Information Technology Test (FIT), is specified in Table 3.2.

A student questionnaire was used to gather student background characteristics, student attitudes, and a description of computer use at school in existing subjects, as well as outside school. Attitude items for this questionnaire are listed in Table 3.3. In addition, a teacher questionnaire was used for collecting information about the content of the lessons as well as classroom practices adopted by teachers of computer education. All questionnaires were highly standardized across educational levels in order to facilitate comparisons between levels.

TABLE 3.2

Items in the Functional Information Technology Test With Reference
to Content Domain

Item Content	Content Domain
1. Dialing a telephone number is an example of input.	Concepts
2. Sorting the names of authors is an example of processing.	Concepts
3. BASIC, PASCAL and LOGO are programming languages.	Concepts
4. The physical parts of a computer are called hardware.	Concepts
5. One can create own software by writing programs.	Concepts
6. A mouse is used for entering instructions into a computer.	Concepts
7. Computer program = instructions to control computer.	Concepts
8. Does very small multimedia computer already exist?	Concepts
9. Data are stored on a disk.	Concepts
10. Permanent storage device for a computer program?	Concepts
11. What happens to a program if a computer is switched off?	Concepts
12. Device giving text you can see and read?	Concepts
13. Why a back-up copy on another diskette is needed?	Computer handling
14. Can interpret instructions on a computer screen?	Computer handling
15. Why persons may need different word processing programs?	Computer handling
16. What is a copy-protected disk?	Computer handling
17. How to restart a computer after freezing?	Computer handling
18. How to fix a problem with a word processor?	Applications
19. Which program is useful for keeping track of a store budget?	Applications
20. Which possibilities are open in a networked computer lab?	Applications
21. Can interpret menu of a word processing program for saving?	Applications
22. Can interpret menu of a word processing program for restart?	Applications
23. Which program is suited for sending similar letters to several people?	Applications
24. Interpretation of spreadsheet screen.	Applications
25. Interpretation of database screen.	Applications
26. Storage device for long periods of time?	Concepts
27. How to load data from storage?	Concepts
28. Why password code is needed?	Computer handling
29. Effect when printer is "offline."	Computer handling
30. What does a cursor do?	Computer handling

Reliability and Validity

As shown in Table 3.4, the reliability of the attitude scales of Relevance and Enjoyment were, in general, acceptable. Elementary school-level reliabilities ranged from .59 to .68. Lower secondary reliabilities ranged from .60 to .84.

As shown in Table 3.5, the reliabilities for the FIT test were low for elementary school students and acceptable for lower secondary school students. In the United States, in particular, the elementary school-level reliability of .47 can be judged to be less than adequate for obtaining consistent measures (DeVellis, 1991).

TABLE 3.3

Attitude Items for Computer Relevance and Enjoyment

Relevance
Computers can help me to learn things more easily.
With computers it is possible to do many practical things.
Knowing how to use computers will help me do well in my career.
Knowing how to use computers is a worthwhile skill.
All students should have an opportunity to learn about computers at school.
It is important for students to learn about computers in order to be informed citizens.
Having computer skills helps you get better jobs.

Enjoyment
I like to talk to others about computers.
Computers can be exciting.
I like reading about computers.
A job using computers would be very interesting.
Computer lessons are a favorite subject for me.
I want to learn a lot about computers.
I like to scan computer journals.
When I pass a computer shop, usually I stop for a while.
Computers interest me little.

TABLE 3.4

Internal Consistency Reliabilities for Computer Relevance and Enjoyment Scales

	Relevance	Enjoyment
Elementary education		
Japan	.66	.67
Netherlands	.59	.68
United States	-	.59
Secondary education		
Japan	.71	.82
Netherlands	.60	.84
United States	.65	.79

MAJOR FINDINGS FROM THE 1989
AND 1992 SURVEYS

The results from CompEd have been reported in numerous publications (see the list of references). Some of the major findings are summarized here.

TABLE 3.5
Internal Consistency Reliabilities for Functional Information Technology Test

	FIT Reliability
Elementary education	
Japan	-
Netherlands	.55
United States	.47
Secondary education	
Japan	.76
Netherlands	.73
United States	.77

There Were Large Differences Between Countries in Access to Computers. Whereas in 1989 all elementary schools surveyed in Canada–British Columbia and the United States were already using computers for instructional purposes (this was also the case for a majority but not all elementary schools in France and New Zealand), other countries were lagging behind. For instance, in Japan just 12% of the elementary schools were using computers; 29% were using computers in Portugal; and 53% were using computers in the Netherlands.

In secondary schools, the situation was usually better, but it was also found at this level that in some countries sizable numbers of schools still did not have computers to be used for instructional purposes. For instance, for lower secondary education (junior high school), 95% of the schools in Greece did not have computers, 56% were lacking computers in Japan, and 45% were without computers in Portugal.

In 1992, 36% of the Japanese elementary schools possessed computers (an increase of 11% compared to 1989), and the Netherlands had an increase from 53% to 83%, whereas in the United States in 1989 all schools surveyed were already equipped with computers. Large increases were also observed for some countries in lower secondary schools. For example, the diffusion rate for Austria increased from 50% to 100%, for Japan from 35% to 71%, and for the Netherlands from 87% to 100%.

There Was Not Enough Hardware and Software in Schools. Based on an analysis of problems experienced by educational practitioners (principals, computer coordinators, and teachers) in 1989, it was concluded that the basic infrastructure for using computers in schools was still viewed as insufficient. Lack of hardware and software for instructional purposes were among the top five of a long list of potential problems in almost every country .

Although in elementary schools in the Netherlands and the United States insufficient availability of hardware was still seen as one of the major problems in 1992, in secondary education there was, across countries, a clear trend that the problem of insufficient number of computers was declining somewhat. Exceptions to this trend were Greek lower secondary schools and upper secondary schools in Japan and Slovenia.

As expected, between 1989 and 1992, the hardware situation in schools improved in terms of numbers of computers. In some countries, such as Japan in secondary education and in the United States, these changes were very substantial. For instance, in Japanese lower secondary school the average number of computers per school increased from 9 to 23, compared to an increase from 18 to 20 in the Netherlands, and from 18 to 24 in the United States. Upper secondary schools in the United States exhibited a very large increase, from an average of 27 to 47 computers per school. Still, with the exception of upper secondary schools in the United States, the numbers of computers in typical schools in countries where the largest numbers of computers were observed, were only large enough to allow for computer use by one complete classroom at a time.

The percentage of 16-bit or larger machines in computer using schools increased over a 3-year period, sometimes by quite a large amount. For instance, the increase was from 7% to 37% in elementary schools in the Netherlands, from 17% to 76% in upper secondary schools in Slovenia, and from 3% to 29% in upper secondary schools in the United States. However, it was also noted that (except for Austria, Japan, and Slovenia) schools apparently still had quite a number of old computers. For instance, the average percentages of 16+ bit machines in elementary and lower secondary schools in the United States for 1992 were just 11% and 17%, respectively. In Austria, Japan, and Slovenia, these percentages were much higher.

As shown in Fig. 3.1, overall availability of instructional tool software in lower secondary schools tended to increase between 1989 and 1992. Exceptions were Greece, and the Netherlands.

There Was Little Integration of Computer Use in the Curriculum of Schools, and Large Differences Existed Between Countries. Computers were, in 1989, mainly used for computer education courses or related activities. That is, in 1989, the main use of computers in schools was teaching students how to use hardware and software. Integration of computers as a tool in the regular school curriculum hardly occurred, which was not surprising, given the lack of available infrastructure, as mentioned previously. The relationship between infrastructural provisions and degree of integration was quite strong, as illustrated in Fig. 3.1. There were large differences in the extent of instructional computing integration among the various nations represented in the study.

There was somewhat more integration of computers into the curriculum in 1992, but not in all countries. Relatively large increases with regard to the integration of computers in the school curriculum were observed between 1989 and 1992 in lower secondary schools in Germany and the Netherlands. Overall, the use of computers in existing school subjects remained limited.

Teachers Were Insufficiently Trained. Teachers are the main gatekeepers in allowing educational innovations to diffuse into the classrooms. Therefore, one of the key factors for effecting an integration of computers in the school curriculum

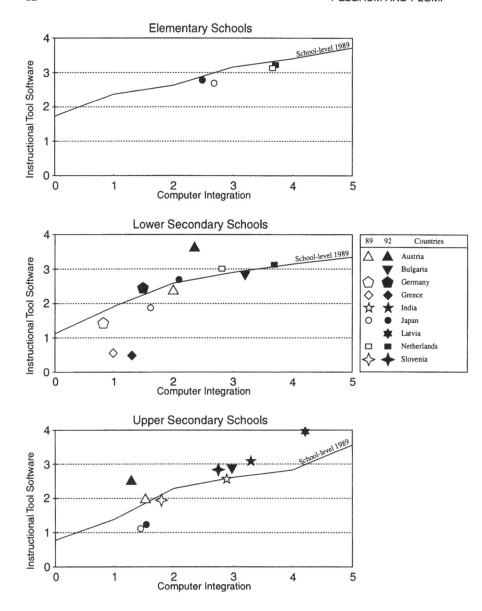

FIG. 3.1.   Country positions and school-level data (for 1989) on degree of computer integration and availability of instructional tool software.

is adequate training of teachers in handling and managing these new tools in their daily practice. The 1989 survey showed that, although many teachers had received some computer related training, most training courses at that time emphasized technical aspects and neglected the pedagogical and didactic aspects of computer applications. The potential benefit of training in these topics was underscored by the finding that degree of integration of computers in school subjects correlated substantially with the amount of emphasis on pedagogical/didactical aspects in the training courses teachers had received. That is, degree of classroom integration of computers was closely tied to extent of training in integration techniques. Between 1989 and 1992 the training needs of teachers increased in elementary education and decreased a little in secondary education.

Not All Students Used Computers, Even in 1992. As shown by Pelgrum, Janssen Reinen, and Plomp (1993), except for Austria and the United States, there were in many countries sizable groups of students who did not use computers at school in the school year 1991–1992. Table 3.6 illustrates that there was still a considerable group of students in Japan and the Netherlands who were not using computers at school in 1992. Although part of these groups may have gained computer experience before the school year 1991–1992, the general implication of these results is that in these countries computers were far from being integrated in the daily (school) life of students.

Students Learned Much About Computers Outside the School. As shown in Fig. 3.2, the FIT scores of students without any access to computers at school did not differ dramatically from students who had access to computers at home only. This finding illustrates that learning outside school can play an important role in preparing youngsters for the information society.

Gender Differences Existed, But Varied Across Countries. Janssen Reinen and Plomp (1993) showed that boys score higher on the FIT test than girls. These differences were substantial in Japan and the Netherlands, but negligible in the United States. With regard to the enjoyment of using computers, these authors

TABLE 3.6
Percentage of Students* in 1991–1992 Using Computers Inside or Outside School

Country	School+ Outside	Only School	Only Outside	Not	At Home	Hours
Elementary Schools						
Japan	11	8	39	42	20	1.2
Netherlands	50	12	27	12	52	3.4
United States	81	12	7	1	42	2.4
Lower Secondary Schools						
Japan	13	19	24	44	21	1.9
Netherlands	60	17	16	6	57	4.0
United States	74	21	2	3	51	2.1

Note. *Students in computer-using schools only.
Source. Adapted from Pelgrum, Janssen Reinen, and Plomp (1993)

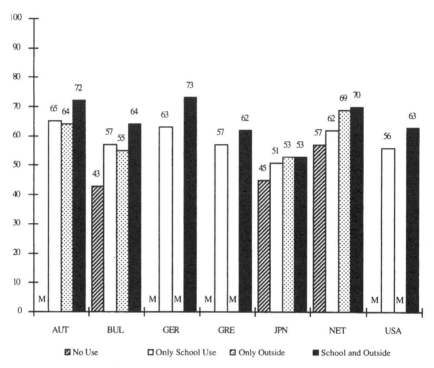

FIG. 3.2.   Percentage correct score on the FIT test by students using computers within and outside school, by country (1992 data).

found that in elementary schools in Japan and the United States these differences hardly existed, whereas in the Netherlands boys liked working with computers much more than girls. These differences become more pronounced (also in Japan and the United States) in secondary schools.

DISCUSSION AND INSIGHTS

A leading principle we have followed in extracting information from the large CompEd databases is the perspective of the student—How and to what extent do students use computers? What do they learn about computers? How do they perceive the relevance of computers and in what context? In this way it is possible to shed some light on the question of how computer use looks when viewed from a global perspective. In the following narrative, we sometimes base our description on interpretation of the results from all countries while focusing especially on the primary and lower secondary levels. For illustrative purposes, tables and figures are limited to data from Japan, the United States, and the Netherlands, because these countries participated in the study at both the elementary and lower secondary levels.

To What Extent and How Do Students Use Computers?

In order to determine whether students used computers at all, they were asked about their use of computers at school and outside school (at home, friends' homes, hobby clubs). This resulted in four possible groups to which students could belong: (a) computer use outside school and at school, (b) only at school, (c) only outside school, and (d) not at all.

Table 3.6 shows that in Japan and the Netherlands, there were sizable groups of students who did not use computers at school in the school year 1991–1992. This indicates that in those countries, computers were far from being integrated in the daily (school) life of all students.

This observation is further confirmed by looking at computer use by students who did have access to computers at school. One may observe in Table 3.7 that in 1992 still a minority of students in Japan used computers more than 10 times a year either in computer classes or for other subjects. Although the percentages for computer education courses in the Netherlands and the United States were much higher than in Japan, use of computers in traditional subjects (such as mathematics, science, and mother tongue) seemed still to be marginal.

Table 3.8 offers some details about the way students used computers at school as of 1992. The most intensive use in elementary schools was playing games (ranked first in all three countries), followed by drill and practice, learning new material,

TABLE 3.7

Percentage of 1991–1992 Students Using Computers at School, and Percentage of Students Who Used Computers 10 or More Times in Specific School Subjects

	Elementary Schools			Lower Secondary Schools		
	Japan	Nether lands	United State	Japan	Nether lands	United States
Computer used	51	67	93	49	78	95
Computer education	17	18	51	10	86	67
Mathematics	5	21	28	2	7	7
Science	1	8	5	2	M	2
Mother tongue	1	24	10	1	7	9
Social studies	3	22	10	1	12	3

Note. M = number of valid cases too small (< 250) or too many missing cases (> 20%).
Source. Adapted from Pelgrum, Janssen Reinen, and Plomp (1993)

TABLE 3.8

Percentage of 1991–1992 Students Using the Computer for a Specific Activity 10
or More Times Per Year

	Japan	Netherlands	United States
Elementary Schools			
Computer used at school	19	62	93
Learning new material	2	9	17
Doing drill and practice	5	19	17
Laboratory experiments	1	3	2
Writing/wordprocessing	3	7	13
Programming assignment	4	3	6
Spreadsheet assignment	0	7	3
Database assignment	0	1	2
Taking tests	0	5	9
Playing games	13	20	53
Lower Secondary Schools			
Computer used at school	32	77	95
Learning new material	2	34	13
Doing drill and practice	1	19	14
Laboratory experiments	1	5	1
Writing/wordprocessing	2	23	21
Programming assignment	2	17	11
Spreadsheet assignment	1	8	7
Database assignment	1	10	5
Taking tests	1	6	4
Playing games	8	14	34

Source. Adapted from Pelgrum, Janssen Reinen, and Plomp (1993)

and word processing (all other uses did not exceed 10% for any country). In lower
secondary schools, the emphasis on word processing was increasing (compared to
elementary education), except for Japan.

Across all countries, it appears that the most regular use of computers in
secondary education was for programming/word processing, followed by learning
new material/drill and practice (see Pelgrum & Plomp, 1993a). Conversely, taking
tests was the least regularly practiced activity. This was also reported earlier by
Pelgrum and Schipper (1993), who found, using 1989 data, that school principals
mentioned test taking as the least practiced type of computer use.

What Do Students Learn and Think About Computers?

Students' knowledge about IT was measured with a 27-item multiple-choice test
(see Table 3.2 for item descriptions) and three attitude scales (of which two, namely
Enjoyment and Relevance are reported here; see Table 3.3). The test was not
administered in Japanese elementary schools, but the attitude scales were. For
greater detail, the reader is referred to Pelgrum and Plomp (1993b).

The extent to which there is overlap between the test and the curriculum to which students were exposed is an important variable in helping in interpreting the international test scores. This measure, which is a composite of teacher judgments about the coverage of the subject matter needed to answer the test items correctly, is referred to here as *coverage*. Graphic representations of student test scores by education system are presented in Fig. 3.3.

It can be observed that in elementary schools in the Netherlands and the United States, the test scores are low. However, although the coverage index in Fig. 3.3 suggests that there is hardly any teaching about the content covered in the test, the

Elementary Schools

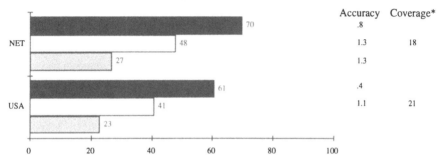

Lower Secondary Schools

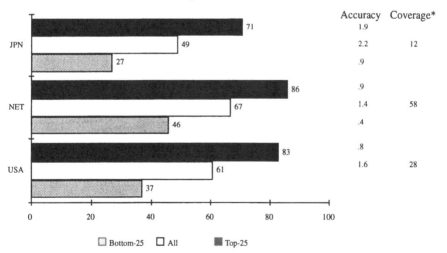

Notes. * = average % coverage of test in teaching.
Accuracy = the sample mean plus/minus this value gives the 95% confidence interval for the population mean based on jackknifed standard error estimate.

FIG. 3.3. Student knowledge of information technology: average percent correct on a 27-item multiple-choice test.

scores certainly indicate that students have learned something, because the average score is well above chance level (which is about 25% correct). For the 25% highest scoring students in Dutch elementary schools, the average percentage correct was 70%, which is well above the average score for lower secondary school students. Reviewing the results of all countries Pelgrum and Plomp (1993b) concluded that:

> In lower secondary education, the highest scores for the total sample occurred in Austria, Germany and the Netherlands. Greece (with an inflated estimate) and the United States [were] holding an intermediate position, while Bulgarian and Japanese students (with on the average 51% and 49% correct) scored the lowest. This trend is the same for the scores of the 25% lowest and highest scoring students. Except for Bulgaria and Japan, the bottom 25% of the students scored well above chance. Chapter 3 showed that the OTL-index[2] differs dramatically between countries varying from less than 20% in Japan to about 90% in Austria. (Pelgrum, Janssen Reinen, & Plomp, 1993, p. 54)

In upper secondary education, the Austrian students have a very high average score on the total test. Latvia, the United States, Slovenia, Bulgaria, and Japan are in a middle position, while the scores for India are quite low, which is not surprising given the large number of students in the sample without exposure to computers. At this level of education, one may also observe great differences between countries with regard to opportunity to learn (Pelgrum & Plomp, 1993b).

Furthermore, Janssen Reinen and Plomp (1993) found that in all countries, boys outperformed girls. They showed that these differences are negligible in some countries (e.g., in the United States), but sizable in other countries (e.g., in Austria). This implies that sustained efforts to promote gender equity with regard to the use of new ITs would probably be effective in countries with sizable gender gaps.

Student Attitudes

As shown in other portions of this book (see chapters 1 and 5), student attitudes toward computers are considered to be very important indicators of students' inclination to adopt this new technology in their lifelong learning. The CompEd study contained a number of attitude scales, of which two are reported here.

Computer Relevance. This scale contained items asking students to indicate their opinion about the relevance of computers for their daily and school life. The second scale contained items about how much they enjoyed working with computers. When looking at the attitude indicators the fairest comparison is a breakdown by different categories of student use (see Fig. 3.4). As for students not using computers the attitude items were more or less hypothetical, not referring to their own practice. Fig. 3.4 shows that the majority of students tended to agree with the relevance of computers. In the United States, the trend from the elementary to

---

[2]OTL stands for the opportunity to learn; the percentage of items from the test covered during student instruction.

Elementary Schools

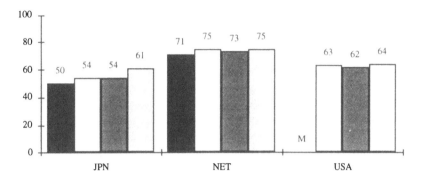

Lower Secondary Schools

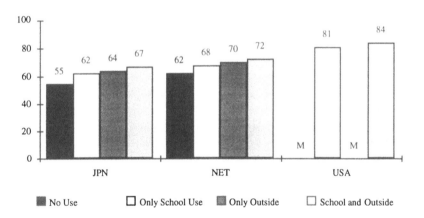

Note. M = number of cases too small ($n < 250$).

FIG. 3.4.   Percentage of 1991–1992 students agreeing that computers are relevant.

the lower secondary level was quite strongly upward, whereas in Japan, the trend was slightly upward, and in the Netherlands, there was a slight downward trend.

Computer Enjoyment.   A comparison between Fig. 3.4 and Fig. 3.5 shows that students tend to agree less with the Enjoyment items than the Relevance items. In Japan, there was a downward trend for students using computers exclusively in school, from elementary to lower secondary school (this trend continues into upper secondary education; see Pelgrum & Plomp, 1993b). On the other hand, interestingly, students using computers exclusively outside school showed an increase in enjoyment as they moved from elementary to lower secondary school. The Dutch

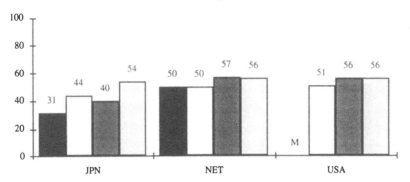

Elementary Schools

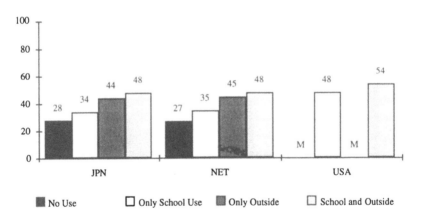

Lower Secondary Schools

Note. M = number of cases too small (*n* < 250)

FIG. 3.5. Percentage of 1991–1992 students agreeing that they enjoy computers.

lower secondary school students seemed to enjoy using computers much less than the elementary schools students. In the United States the trend is also downward, but not as strong. These downward trends should be taken as serious indicators that, overall, school does not seem to increase students' motivation to work with computers.

SOME REFLECTIONS

The following general conclusions are based on the combined results of Phase 1 (1987–1990) and Phase 2 (1990–1993) studies:

There is Wide-Scale Implementation of IT at the School Level, But Not at the Classroom Level. The CompEd data show that in most of the participating countries computers have gained their place in the schools. In many countries (almost) all schools not only have computers, but also use computers for various purposes. This means that in industrialized countries it is almost impossible to imagine schools without computers.

Unfortunately, this general trend does not apply to every classroom. In 1992, there were still many teachers who were not using and were not ready to use computers as an integral part of their teaching. A nice illustration of this is provided by ten Brummelhuis and Plomp (1994), based on the CompEd data from the Netherlands. The researchers were able to show that the increase from 1989 to 1992 in computer-using teachers in specific subject areas was (in more than 90% of the cases) in schools that in 1989 had no teacher in that particular subject using the computer. This illustrates that there is no further diffusion within the schools, but rather more schools where a single or a few teachers started to use computers.

Because Schools Tend to Start With "Easy" Computer Use, There is Danger That Full Integration of Computers Will Not Be Achieved. The fact that schools are starting with "easy" usage can be illustrated in two ways. First of all, the CompEd data show that "teaching and learning about computers" is the most widespread computer use. This is an easy application, as it asks for only a few teachers to be trained in computer education, although it does not demand computer integration into the existing subject areas in the school curriculum.

A second illustration of "easy" application is the fact that the types of computer use most applied in schools are tutor-mode applications, such as drill and practice and tutorials. More complex applications, directed at problem solving and independent learning by students, are rarely applied, even though it is these applications that are challenging teachers to change their didactical approaches and their own roles.

Although we would be the last to say that a strategy of starting with "easy" applications is wrong, with reference to the phenomenon previously mentioned, we think there is a chance that schools and teachers will not proceed from the easy applications to full utilization of the potentials of the new technologies.

Insufficient Hardware Infrastructure Will Limit the Implementation of Computers and, in General, Technology in Education. The CompEd data show that in many countries schools do have enough computers to let even one classroom of students work with computers all at the same time. Imagine what would happen if all teachers in the school wanted to fully integrate computers into instruction. Given the present hardware infrastructure, it would be practically impossible. As it is not yet realistic to expect (in the short term) that all students will have their own computer at school, one has to be realistic about the expectation of technology diffusion into instruction. Schools must become creative in organizing the use of limited resources, both in scheduling students' activities outside regular classrooms, and in utilizing the possibilities that some students can use computers in their homes.

Computer Use and Computer Education in Schools are Important From an Equity Perspective. Because there are still many students who do not possess or are not using computers at home, the school will continue to be an important environment to get students involved in and motivated to use computers. This is not only important from the perspective of improving the quality of instruction, but also from the perspective of preparing students for a future profession or democratic citizenship. Because computers have their place in all aspects of society, they must have a self-evident place in the daily school life. It is the example of everyday use in school that makes the computer a natural tool in the hands of students.

REFERENCES

Alreck, P., & Settle, R. (1985). *The survey research handbook.* Homewood, IL: Irwin.

Brummelhuis, A. C. A., ten, & Plomp, Tj. (1994). Computers in primary and secondary education: The interest of an individual teacher or a school policy? *Computers and Education, 22*(4), 291–299.

DeVellis, R. F. (1991). *Scale development: Theory and applications.* Newbury Park, CA: Sage.

Janssen Reinen, I., & Plomp, Tj. (1993). Gender and computers: Another area of inequity in education? In W. J. Pelgrum, I. Janssen Reinen, & Tj. Plomp (Eds.), *Schools, teachers, students and computers: A cross-national perspective.* The Hague: International Association for the Evaluation of Educational Achievement.

Pelgrum, W. J., Janssen Reinen, I., & Plomp, Tj. (Eds.). (1993). *Schools, teachers, students and computers: A cross-national perspective.* The Hague: International Association for the Evaluation of Educational Achievement.

Pelgrum, W. J., & Plomp, Tj. (Eds.). (1993a). *The IEA study of computers in education: Implementation of an innovation in 21 education systems.* Oxford, UK: Pergamon Press.

Pelgrum, W. J., & Plomp, Tj. (1993b). What do students know, learn and think about computers? In W. J. Pelgrum, I. Janssen Reinen, & Plomp, Tj. (Eds.), *Schools, teachers, students and computers: A cross-national perspective.* The Hague: International Association for the Evaluation of Educational Achievement.

Pelgrum, W. J., & Schipper A. T. (1993) Indicators of computer integration in education. *Computers in Education, 21,* 141–149.

Chapter 4

Information Technology and Children From a Classroom Perspective

Betty A. Collis
Kwok-Wing Lai

Information technology (IT), primarily involving the application of computers in the educational setting, is perceived by educators and the public in countries throughout the world as capable of having a significant effect on the developing child. The study of this effect—what mediates it and how it may be channeled to the best advantage of the child—is a topic of major interest to researchers, teachers, and educational decision makers throughout the world.

Despite this extensive interest in the impact of computers in education, it remains difficult to draw conclusions from the experiences that are occurring. This is partly because the IT field is continually changing in its characteristics; but more importantly it is because "the effect" of computer use cannot be expressed in a straightforward fashion, but instead must be considered in the context of the complicated network of variables in which the use is embedded (Collis, 1988; McGee, 1987; Salomon, 1990). These variables include characteristics of the computer use itself, such as software types and design aspects, as well as hardware variations. They also include variables related to various characteristics of the students and teachers involved, and of teacher decision making, including how effectively the teacher integrates computer use into a meaningful learning experience for the child. The social interaction between student and student and between teacher and student also influences the impact of computer use in school (Feldman, 1989; Tharp, 1989). In addition, school, regional, and national culture also are part of the system of influences, as culture in its various manifestations embeds and shapes the system and the subsequent result of computer use (Peled, Peled, & Alexander, 1989).

43

Despite these challenges, there is a consensus that research into the impact of computer use on children's cognitive functioning must be done, but done in a way that is sensitive to the system of variables that shape and are shaped by it. In response to this challenge, UNESCO, the Bulgarian Ministry of Science and Higher Education, the Bulgarian National Neuroscience and Behavior Research Program and other sponsors representing researchers from 19 countries collaborated in a major cross-cultural research project, called Information Technology in Education and Children (ITEC). The ITEC Project formally began in May 1988 at an international meeting in Bulgaria initiated by UNESCO and finished its analysis and reporting in 1992. Sixteen countries were actively involved throughout the study as settings for school observations.

In this chapter, we briefly describe this project, including its conceptual, methodological, and organizational evolution. We describe the data-gathering and analysis procedures in the study and summarize its major findings. From the ITEC experience, we conclude with some observations about the ambition of conducting an international study investigating the impact of computer use in school on children's thinking and reasoning performance.

OVERVIEW OF THE ORGANIZATIONAL
HISTORY OF ITEC

Project Background, Prior to May 1988

Because of the scientific expertise in Bulgaria with respect to the new area of computer use in education, a relationship with UNESCO was developed in which initiatives related to international exploration of this area could be stimulated. In this context, the First International Conference, "Children in the Information Age" was held in Bulgaria, in May 1985. This conference was organized by the (former) Lyudmila Zhivkova International Foundation, with assistance from UNESCO, the International Institute for Applied Systems Analysis, the (Bulgarian) State Committee for Science and Technical Progress, and the Education Ministry of Bulgaria. In response to recommendations unanimously adopted by the participants at this conference, preparations began for an international scientific project entitled, "Children in the Information Age," to be cosponsored by UNESCO and other international organizations and institutes. One aspect of this project was to be the execution of "an international comparative study of the psychological consequences of computer introduction in the world of children of different cultures and traditions."

The 23rd session of the UNESCO General Conference adopted a proposal to include this overall initiative which included the aforementioned research project, in its planned intergovernmental information program.

The second "Children in the Information Age" Conference was held, May 1987. Later in 1987, an initial planning meeting was held in Bulgaria to further discuss the international comparative study of the long-term effects on child development of the use of computers. A first draft of a project proposal was prepared and circulated by UNESCO to a core group of international researchers, for comment and consideration. Several experts were then invited to a new meeting, in Bulgaria, in May 1988.

ITEC Project Initiation, 1988 to 1989

Under the support of the Lyudmila Zhivkova International Foundation, the Committee for Science of the Bulgarian Council of Ministers, and UNESCO, the "International Expert Meeting" was held in Tolboukhin, Bulgaria, May 1988. Thirty-two researchers from 14 countries participated in this meeting. During this meeting, the name ITEC was born, and major decisions about the design, theoretical framework, research questions, variables of interest, and the methodology of the project were discussed and agreed, at least in their first versions. Major aspects of these decisions—those that remained steady during the project and those that changed over time—are discussed later in this chapter. Assen Jablensky (then a professor at the Bulgarian Medical Academy) and Betty Collis (then at the University of Victoria, Canada, and now at the University of Twente, the Netherlands) were invited to serve as coprincipal investigators of the project, and the preliminary organization of the project began.

The initial step was the preparation of the first project overview (May 1988) and a series of 11 "working papers" relating to key project issues. (This overview and the 11 working papers are available in the full Final Report of the ITEC Project; Collis, 1993.)

The second ITEC planning meeting was held in Sofia, Bulgaria, January 1989. During this meeting, the theoretical framework for the study was further delineated, and based on the analysis that had gone on during the previous 6 months, a revision of the research schedule planning and methodology of the project was worked out.

Following this, a first invitation to participate in the project was formally circulated, and the intentions of the project were presented at the UNESCO International Congress, "Education and Informatics: Strengthening International Cooperation," Paris, April 1989. The third ITEC project planning meeting was held, shortly after, in Sofia, Bulgaria, May 1989. The 15 researchers at this meeting made further refinements and decisions about project planning, variables and research questions, timeline and responsibilities, and expectations for national leaders. A major decision made at this meeting was to change the planned design of the project from a 3-year longitudinal comparative study to a two-phase approach, in which Phase 1 would be a pilot and exploratory study. This design change is discussed further in this chapter.

Formal letters of invitation were sent to potential national leaders and intensive communication concerning national participation took place during the period, June 1989 to October 1989. A new version of the Project Planning Document was prepared, a "Steering Committee" (six persons) and a project "Methodological Advisor" were appointed, and national teams and Chief Collaborating Investigators for each participating country were established. As of November 1989, project teams consisting of researchers, schools, and teachers had been established in Bulgaria, Canada, China, Costa Rica, France, Hungary, Israel, Japan, Mexico, Netherlands, New Zealand, Portugal, Romania, Sweden, United States, Russia, and Zimbabwe. Twenty-four schools and 27 classroom teachers were selected for involvement. (Portugal later withdrew.)

The next ITEC planning meeting was held in Bulgaria, November 1989. Out of this meeting came the 40 pages of specific observation and interview instruments for Phase 1, the requirements for standardized videotaping of computer-use lessons, and other requirements for the national teams. Final timelines for Phase 1 data collection and analysis were established and materials were sent to all national teams.

ITEC Phase 1: Organizational Procedures

Preliminary descriptive materials were accumulated and a first summary report done for the 24 schools participating in Phase 1 during the period January through March 1990 (during this period, Portugal was still participating). This preliminary summary involved overall descriptions of the schools, interviews with the principal in each school, information on all the participating students (approximately 660), information about the teachers and interviews with the teachers, and summaries of 15-minute descriptive videotapes of each class and school.

Researchers began their observations of computer-use sessions in the participating classes during March and April 1990. Another project meeting was scheduled, in Bulgaria, May 1990. At this meeting, procedures for coding the videotapes were finalized. The three computer-use observations and videotaping and teacher interviews were completed by all the schools by August 1990. Extensive documentation, field notes, observational data, and summary comments were submitted to UNESCO in 1992 and distributed internationally in 1993 (Collis, 1993).

Because of several factors, including some radical political changes in the central and eastern European countries participating in ITEC during the period 1988 to 1992 and changes in the research responsibilities of many of the researchers, the infrastructure needed to support a continuation of the ITEC Project beyond its Phase 1 has not been materialized.

CONCEPTUAL AND METHODOLOGICAL ISSUES IN ITEC

General Rationale for the Study

During the project launch in May 1988 a number of fundamental conceptual decisions were made. Some of these decisions remained throughout its subsequent course, whereas others were modified. The objective of the project was to "involve the systematic examination of interactions among factors influencing the effects of IT on children's cognitive development using common variables, methodologies, and instrumentation and through simultaneous focus on children in specific age groups in countries throughout the world" (Collis, 1993, p. 4). This core intention never changed. It was also agreed that the study should involve common definitions and operationalizations of its salient dependent and independent variables, should use common data-capturing instruments and procedures, and should "maintain an appropriate respect for the naturally occurring differences in embedding school, social, and cultural environments" (p. 5) that interact with any computer experiences that the child may have. Although this appropriate respect remained throughout the project, and operational consensus was reached on many of the key contextual variables that were studied, the quest for a concise and cross-culturally valid measure to represent higher level cognitive development did not reach a resolution (at least, not in terms of "concise" and "measurable"). It was also agreed that brief, episodic interventions involving technology were not likely to have a lasting and meaningful impact on children's higher level cognitive development, and thus adequate time had to be allowed for repeated child–computer interactions in natural classroom settings to occur. This recognition was maintained throughout the project, but was reflected not through a long-term intervention but by studying classrooms where child–computer interactions were already well established. The importance of culture as a contextual variable was to be reflected in a cross-national approach. This certainly was maintained throughout the project.

The initial project assumptions were summarized in May 1988 around six points:

1. The general interest of the study will be the relationships between the use of IT in education and children's cognitive and metacognitive development.
2. The study will be international and will involve a general framework of cross-cultural comparisons.
3. The study will involve the use of a variety of applications of IT within the school setting.
4. The study will consider the child in the context of his or her environment—as defined by variables relating to teacher characteristics, instructional strategies, school, family, cultural, and computer-use characteristics. It is accepted that change in aspects of any of these variable clusters can influence the overall system encompassing the variables, and therefore that a consideration of the child in isolation with a computer is not appropriate.
5. The study will be longitudinal.
6. The study will involve a core set of common research questions, variables, instruments, and other measurement techniques, applied to a same-age cohort at specific points in time identical in each culture (Collis, 1993, p. 5).

Of these initial premises of the study, all were, with some permutations, maintained. Also, the conceptual core of the study, the importance of social interaction for children's cognitive development as articulated in the theoretical work of the Russian psychologist Vygotsky (1966/ 1986, 1978), remained throughout, as did the awareness of interacting variables expressed in Item 4. However, how to express this theoretical framework in terms of a manageable set of measurable variables was a topic of considerable debate during the 1988 to 1990 period. Many variables that the researchers agreed were influential with respect to children's higher level cognitive development, such as family circumstances and dynamics, came to be unwieldy in terms of standardized international assessment and compromises had to be made as to how to find a common system of categorization valid over diverse communities and cultures. The following passages, taken from a 1990 project document, indicate the theoretical framework finally agreed on as the basis of subsequent measurement and analysis in the study (Collis, 1993, pp. 118–121).

Conceptual Core for the Study

The conceptual starting point for the study was derived from the theoretical work of the Soviet psychologist, Vygotsky. Vygotsky emphasized the important role that social interaction plays in cognitive development (Gallimore & Goldenberg, 1989; Schoenfeld, 1989; Vygotsky, 1966/1986, 1978; Wertsch, 1985). Vygotsky (1978) hypothesized that an episode of cognitive development emerges through two cycles: "First, it appears on the social plane and then on the psychological plane. First it appears between people as an inter-psychological category, and then within the child as an intra-psychological category" (p. 163). "Learning in context" is seen as the motive force for cognitive development, and thus the analysis of children's thinking and learning cannot be separated from the analysis of the social organization in which the learning transactions occur (Levine, 1988; Schoenfeld, 1989; Zimmerman, Smith, Bastone, & Friend, 1989). Vygotskyan theory, therefore, gave the project its rationale for the expectation that computer use, embedded as it is in the social context of the school and cultural setting, can affect the child's higher level cognitive functioning (see also, Perret-Clermont & Schubauer-Leoni, 1989; Tikhomirov, 1988). Vygotskyan theory also underscores the necessity of studying the complex of variables pertaining to teacher and student interaction with regard to computer use in any consideration of the eventual effect of such use.

Multidimensional Aspects of Computer Impact on Children's Cognitive Development

Vygotsky's theories were not the only source of support for a multidimensional approach to the study of computers in education on children's metacognitive development. The extensive research that had already been conducted on aspects of the impact of computers in education substantiated the conclusion that such impact cannot be considered in isolation; it is inextricably embedded in and covaries with a large number of other variables (Clark, 1985; Collis, 1988; Eraut & Hoyles, 1988; Hawkins & Sheingold, 1986). Technological innovations are "interpreted and shaped by the knowledge, experience, and setting of those teachers and students who encounter them" (Hawkins & Sheingold, 1986, p. 43) and "serve as mirrors of the minds and cultures" in which they live (Pea & Sheingold, 1986, p. 10).

Many clusters of variables have been studied, as critically mediating the impact of computer use on children's learning. Elaborations of clusters were compiled from a number of sources, including Cox, Rhodes, and Hall (1988), and Gayeski (1989), among many others (see Collis, 1993, p. 119, for an elaboration). From the research base and after discussions among the ITEC researchers, the following key contextual variables were focused on with ITEC:

- Family socioeconomic and educational levels
- Child's ability level
- Child's prior experiences and understanding with computers
- Child's gender
- Teacher's subject matter expertise and pedagogical skill
- Teacher's expertise with computer use in the classroom
- Teacher's attitudes and self-confidence about computer use
- Teacher's preferred instructional style
- Level of support available to the teacher with respect to computer use
- Availability and location of computers within the school
- School climate relative to technology
- Support of the principal
- Regional and national culture with respect to technology
- Type of computer use
- Frequency of computer use
- Software design characteristics
- Teacher–student interaction patterns
- Student–student interaction patterns
- Curriculum and student relevance of computer use
- Lesson integration of computer use

This sort of multifactorial system allowed us to investigate, not the impact of computer use on children's higher level cognitive development, but instead the combinations of factors that are most likely to be associated with productive metacognitive activity. This was a direction being endorsed by others as most productive for current research in the impact of computers in education (Phi Delta Kappa, 1987; see also Perkins & Salomon, 1989).

Research Questions

In the context of the theoretical framework presented here and after 2 years of iteration and discussion among the geographically dispersed research team, the following general research questions were finally accepted for the project:

- In the context of various combinations of background variables, under what combinations of characteristics of computer use, social interaction surround-

ing computer use, and instructional integration of computer use is a positive impact on children's higher level cognitive functioning more likely to occur?
• How do these sets of conditions vary in different cultures and countries?

Arriving at these research questions took compromise and much discussion. (The original set of research questions suggested for the project at its start-up in May 1988 were broader both in scope—"What factors facilitate or constrain the diffusion of IT usage in schools? How does the family both affect and be affected by the use of different types of IT in education?"—and in ambition "Are there measurable cognitive, metacognitive, and social effects on child development that are associated with the use of different applications of IT in education?") Continual trade-offs were made between simplification and manageability, and scientific integrity and impact. For example, "Culture" proved very difficult to operationalize, and we finally decided to equate "culture" first with country, and then with "school–class–teacher grouping" in our analyses. Thus, we basically collected data by classroom units, and did not find a better way to conceptualize and operationalize "culture" as an influence. Also, we ended up doing virtually nothing with family variables, because of the complexity of dealing with such variables in a systematic way in a multicountry study. Again for reasons of complexity and sensitivity, we recorded nothing about the overall competency, intelligence, or imagination of the teachers involved, although we knew these variables make a critical difference in whatever happens in the school setting.

Thus, although it was agreed that a simple cause-and-effect approach ("What is the effect of computer use on children's higher level cognitive development?", with "computer use" being the independent variable and "higher level cognitive development" the dependent variable) was not possible, our recognition of the complexity of the issue also prevented us from finding an easy-to-articulate and straightforward focus for our project and analyses. Because we realized there would be no simple "answer" forthcoming from our investigations, we could see that our project was not going to generate a "result" that could quickly capture attention or have "statistically significant results."

This resulted in a scientific tension throughout the project. Should we use an "action research" or qualitative approach, where we focus on a better understanding of system and process, rather than an approach in which the causal impact of computer use was specifically under investigation? (For an elaboration of "formative experiments" as a sort of action research, see Newman, 1990.) But if we do this, what do we do with the "rich" mountain of observation data, field notes, and increasing complexity that emerges? How can we synthesize and make sense out of what we accumulate? Shouldn't we have some sort of pretest/posttest, control group aspect? Shouldn't we be getting "results"? Many of the national funding agencies involved with the project expected causal results in order to commit funds and support to the project, and also some of the researchers themselves would have preferred an hypothesis-testing approach, in which a control group, not using computers, was compared to an experimental group using computers, and pre–post comparisons would be used to test an hypothesis of impact of computer use on higher level cognitive development.

This debate over an appropriate methodology for the study led to the major evolution in the project, from an expectation that the study could be carried out via a quasi-experimental design in which control groups in each country not using computers in school would be compared longitudinally with experimental groups using computers, to a so-called two-phase design, which is discussed later in this chapter. It also confronted us with the "dependent variable" problem, to be discussed in the subsequent section, as it was discussed continually throughout the project.

The "Dependent Variable" Problem

Clearly, we had difficulties selecting and operationalizing the context variables for our study, but these difficulties were not as substantial as those related to the "dependent variable" of the research—children's higher level cognitive functioning. Everyone agreed such functioning was what we wanted to focus on (rather than a target such as, e.g., "improvement in mathematics skills"), because of the belief, or hope, throughout the world that computer use might have a particularly valuable influence on "higher level" thinking processes, such as problem solving, or critical thinking, or metacognitive strategies. This, however, relates to the major complexity of our study: What did we really mean by "higher level cognitive functioning"? Take the term *metacognition* as an example. In one typical example from the many reviews we collected, *metacognition* is defined as "the conscious attention to and control of one's process and progress in a learning task" ("Metacognition," 1987, p. 13), but also as "thinking about and being aware of one's thinking and involves self-monitoring, regulation, evaluation, and direction of cognitive activity" (p. 13). So the term *metacognition* refers to both the knowledge of one's own thought processes and the regulation and control of these processes. However, in contrast, Perkins and Salomon (1989) defined *cognitive skills* as "general gripping devices for retrieving and wielding domain specific knowledge, as hands that need to configure to the kind of knowledge in question" (p. 23). How can we operationalize these concepts and measure them, validly and reliably, so that we could see how "metacognitive development" was affected by computer-use situations? Would whatever definition we use or any procedure we choose for measurement be meaningful and manageable in a cross-cultural study? The "dependent variable" problem was another reason for our two-phase design evolution.

The Two-Phase Design and the Research Targets for Phase 1

The major change in planning for our study was taken in May 1989, when, after much discussion and exploration, we decided that our original intention of some sort of quasi-experimental comparison of computer-using and noncomputer-using classrooms relative to changes in children's higher level cognitive functioning could not, with scientific integrity, take place until at least a first phase of systematic exploration occurred. Thus, the idea of a two-phase design was accepted, with Phase 1 having the following preliminary research questions, seen as necessary antecedents for addressing the general research questions of the study:

• In the context of children using computers in the classroom, what are measurable or at least observable indicators of presumed "higher level cognitive functioning"?
• Do these indicators vary cross-culturally?
• If the cross-cultural variation in the indicators of "higher level cognitive functioning" is not too great, can a reliable methodology, usable in countries around the world, be found to measure the appearance and change of these indicators over time and in the complex context of the computer-use setting?

Based on the results of these preliminary investigations, it was hoped that at the end of Phase 1, we would be able to:

• Generate a hypothesis based on our general research question for comparative testing in Phase 2 of the study.
• Refine the methodology relative to the special needs of a multinational study.
• More sharply define the set of relevant contextual variables.
• Reach consensus about an operational definition of the outcome variable, "higher level cognitive functioning."

Other Methodological Decisions

Many other design issues confronting ITEC could also be discussed here, but because of limitations of time and space, only two are briefly mentioned (a full discussion appears in Collis, 1993). The two issues mentioned here relate to the selection of a sample for Phase 1, and to the use of videotaping as one of our data collection strategies.

Teachers. It was decided for Phase 1 to seek out existing classrooms in participating countries in which a teacher of 9- and 10-year-old children had a reputation of doing "good, interesting things" on a regular basis in terms of computer use with children in his or her instructional setting. We made this choice in order to maximize the chance of finding measurable, observable indicators of higher level cognitive functioning by making the teacher variable as controlled (and strong) as possible. This decision was also made in order to somewhat control the variables relating to teacher experience with computers, teacher attitude about computer use and about innovation in instruction, availability of computers and usable software, school and community support for computer use, and experience of the students involved with computer use in an instructional setting. The decision was also made for a practical reason—the project had no funding to set up computer use situations in "ordinary classrooms," and no funding or time to train teachers in some sort of internationally consistent manner. Thus, we moved from an interventionist to a naturalistic approach, and consequently lost even more any margin of hope we might have had of "showing" the effect of computer use on children's cognitive functioning, at least during Phase 1. We also recognized the limitations of generalization with such a sample selection procedure, as we had predominantly good, imaginative, exceptional teachers and exceptional school situations in our sample. However, from this sample we could use a "backward mapping approach" (Fullan, Miles, & Anderson, 1988) to address the preliminary research questions for Phase 1.

Videotaping. Another methodological decision we made was to supplement our various observation and interview procedures with a standardized protocol for videotaping school and computer-use situations (see, e.g., Schoenfeld, 1989, for a discussion of the value of videotape analysis when a team of researchers are working on a broadscale research study). From this decision, we accumulated approximately 100 video fragments, each of about 15 minutes—in general, 4 per participating class. These include in-depth observations of at least three separate classroom lessons involving computer use of the type that the teacher felt would be likely to stimulate what he or she believed to be valuable higher level cognitive functioning on the part of the students. (Each researcher was left to work out with the teacher what these computer activities might be.) For each observation, structured videotaping was done of the overall classroom environment in which the computer use occurred; other aspects of the lesson before, during, and after the computer use; and teacher–student and student–student interactions before, during, and after the computer use. Following each in-depth observation, a detailed interview was conducted with the classroom teacher, in which he or she discussed the behaviors or other indicators of higher level cognitive functioning in the children that the teacher felt occurred during the lesson. Following this interview, a written analysis was done by the researcher as to the extent to which he or she agreed with the teacher's appraisal of possible higher level cognitive functioning among the students. We then developed and validated coding procedures for the videotapes based on the "mapping-sentence technique" (see Peled, 1993), and attempted to use them to triangulate the teacher and researcher reports of indicators of "higher level cognitive functioning." Using the videotapes added to the richness and complexity of the data collected for the study, but also added considerable time and analysis loads on the researchers.

Other Instrumentation

A 40-page battery of observation instruments and interview forms was sent to each national leader at the beginning of 1990. This battery consisted of 12 forms, each with its own procedures for data collection. The forms were first circulated among the participating researchers, for pilot validation and comment. The forms were as follows:

Form A: General sample description, relating to demographic information about each participating school, teacher, and class, including prior experiences with computers.

Form B: General description of the school and its culture, including an overall description of the school, and more detailed information about the school's experiences with computers.

Form C: Interview protocol for the school principal.

Form D: Student information, including the teacher's responses to various questions about each child, and responses from each student relating to his or her feelings about solving problems and learning new skills.

Form E: Interview protocol with the teacher, including information about the teacher's teaching experience and methods, and his or her use of computers with the children involved in the ITEC study.

Form F1: Transcript and summary of the descriptive videotape, relating to the 15-minute videotape of the school, its neighborhood, and the teacher and class in noncomputer activities.

Form F2: Summaries of the computer-use lessons, including summary information about the students' engagement with computers during the lessons.

Form G: Researcher's summaries of the computer-use settings, during the videotaped computer-use lessons, including specifics of hardware and software, an instructional overview of each lesson, and observations concerning the quantity and quality of student–student and student–teacher interaction during each lesson.

Form H: Transcript and summary sheets for the three computer-use lessons.

Form I: Interview protocol with the teacher, relating to the teacher's impression of higher level thinking displayed by the students while engaged in computer use.

Form J: Researcher's summary of the computer-use activity, including any comments pertinent to the study.

Form K: Coding forms for the videotapes.

In addition, each researcher was asked to prepare an in-depth report on his or her experiences with the project, including a summary of the motivations of those involved for participating in the project, the researcher's own impressions of behaviors assumed to demonstrate higher level cognitive activity related to computer use, and the researcher's own suggestion for a response to ITEC's general and preliminary research questions.

All these forms, as well as information about their development and validation, are described in full in the final report (Collis, 1993). All classroom-observation data was collected during the period January through June 1990, and completed sets of forms were returned by the researchers by the end of 1990.

Has all this careful effort accomplished our Phase 1 goal of better conceptuali-
zation and measurement of our "elusive" dependent variable? We comment on this
following a summary of the results of the data collection in the next section.

RESULTS

In this section, we present a sampling of results from the various observation and
interview forms. We then combine these results to address the preliminary questions
for Phase 1 and also the ITEC general research questions.

General Sample Description

Twenty-two schools from 16 countries completed a full participation in the study.
Of the 16 countries, Mexico had 4 schools; Romania, France, and Costa Rica had
2 schools each, and the remaining countries—Bulgaria, Canada, China, Hungary,
Israel, Japan, the Netherlands, New Zealand, Russia, Sweden, the United States,
and Zimbabwe—had 1 school each. There was one participating class from each
school, and one participating teacher per class, with the exception of Hungary and
Japan, where there were two teachers involved with each of the participating classes.
However, only one teacher per class was included in the analysis. There were
approximately 680 children involved (over the year of data collection, there was
some fluctuation in total student numbers); the mean number of students per class
was 30; the children were almost all in the age range 9 to 10 years; they and their
classes were not judged as exceptional relative to other children and schools in their
regions with regard to noncomputer-related characteristics. In 17 of the 22 classes,
more than half of the children had previously experienced computer use in schools.
Of the teachers, 9 were males and 14 were females, with an average of 15.7 years
of teaching experience. Nineteen of the teachers had some training with regard to
educational computer use, generally with some exposure to word processing,
educational computer games, and other types of software, to the use of drawing
software, and to fundamentals of BASIC and LOGO programming. However, the
nature and extent of the teachers' training experiences varied widely and often was
only very limited.

From the overall analysis of the demographic data, it could be said that, other
than being in a school where computers had been provided for young children and
a class where the teacher was already making use of computers, the children,
teachers, and schools in the ITEC project were not exceptional in any particular
characteristic.

A Closer Look at the ITEC Schools

- In the ITEC final report, 24 pages are required to summarize the contextual
  variables pertinent to the ITEC schools (Collis, 1993, pp. 138–162). High-
  lights of this summary include:

- The schools were almost all public schools, located in major cities, and often could be described as middle-class in terms of parents' educational levels.
- Although in 12 of the 22 schools fewer than 10% of the children had computers at home, and in 16 of the schools fewer than 10% of the teaching staff had computers at home, the schools themselves had more computers than normal for schools in their countries, with 17 schools being in the top 25% of schools nationally and 4 schools being near the average.
- The computers themselves (296 among the 22 schools) were in many different locations within the schools, and of varying types and ages.
- The schools made a variety of uses of their computers, with all of them indicating that the computers were used as objects of study in themselves, as well as tools and, with more diversity, for use with specific educational software.
- Despite having relatively superior computer resources compared to other schools in their countries, fewer than 10% of the teachers in the schools were making use of the school computer resources.

Thus, the ITEC schools were different in that, for a large variety of reasons, they had managed to acquire an exceptional amount of computer resources (relative to other elementary schools at that time). The ITEC teachers were unusual in that they were making use of the computer resources. Apart from this, there was no particular pattern in where the computers were located or how they were used or in the characteristics of the software that were used.

Principals' Opinions About Computer Use

The school leader is a central figure in deciding what and how computers are being used in the school. The amount of computer resources the ITEC schools had showed that the school principals were supportive in computer use. The interviews with each of the school principals were carefully translated and coded, by two different teams of ITEC researchers, and the results compared and verified (see Collis, 1993, pp. 163–180). As a summary of these interviews:

- The principals believed that computers in their schools were bringing positive benefits to the schools, although they gave many different illustrations of what these positive benefits were. Most frequently stated was the belief that computers raise the enthusiasm of the students.
- The majority of the principals felt there was not enough good software available. They indicated little concern about the costs associated with computer use or organizational issues relating to computer use and maintenance.
- The principals agreed that teacher training was a major concern.
- The principals felt that computers could be of benefit to all students, at all ages, and saw no particular target group for whom the computers would be most, or least, appropriate.

- The principals were already satisfied with the quality of student–student and student–teacher interactions in their schools and saw no reason to fear that computer use would diminish this quality. They were not looking to technology to compensate for poor conditions in their schools, but to take advantage of opportunities for strategic development.

Thus, the fact that the principals of the ITEC schools were unanimously positive about their schools, and about the benefits of computers in those schools was probably a key factor in making the schools exceptional in terms of computer experiences available to at least some classes of children. What those benefits were varied and tended to be expressed in global terms, but were seen as good for all students.

Summary of the ITEC Students

Although the ITEC students were described by their teachers as predominately average in their families' socioeconomic levels, and predominately average in their academic achievement levels, the majority of them were described as very interested in computers. A wide range of computer-use activities were being engaged in by the children, including word processing, the use of drill and practice programs and other sorts of educational software, BASIC and LOGO programming activities, educational games, and the use of drawing and graphing programs. The teachers saw no tendency to favor individual or group work on the part of the children.

The students described themselves as not likely to give up easily when a task is hard, as preferring to find their own ways to solve problems rather than being given instructions, as sometimes getting irritated if someone revealed how to solve a problem while they were still trying to work it out, and as offering to help their friends with problems. In general, the attitudes of the students toward problem-solving situations could be described as positive. Although causality with respect to computer use cannot be claimed for these positive problem-solving attitudes, the fact that these were computer-using children and that they apparently felt good about themselves as problem solvers was a pleasing correlation, and one that spanned the many different cultures and countries and ways of using computers represented in the study.

Summary of Teachers' Interviews

Other than being enthusiastic users of computers with their classes, there were no particular similarities among the teachers in terms of their ages, years of experience, training, and ways of using computers for instructional purposes. There were many differences in teaching style, in who the teacher turned to for support and help, in the sort of training and computer-use experiences the teachers have had. However, there were also a number of similarities among the teachers:

- Most took their students to a computer laboratory for their computer use.
- Most supervised their students themselves when the students were using computers.
- Like their principals, most felt that there was benefit for all types of students with computers.
- All believed there were many benefits that could come to their students through computer use, but like their principals, they varied widely on the types of benefits cited (in this case, 26 different categories of benefits were identified, with the one being mentioned most often, "it would help independent work," which was named by 7 of the 23 teachers).

The teachers were divided as to whether they had changed the way lessons were taught or organized because of the computer. Of the 13 who answered yes, many felt that their lessons had become more student-centered, with more time for individualized instruction. However, a number of the teachers felt that the computer affected the classroom atmosphere rather than their individual styles of teaching, with the computer being simply another tool integrated into their existing instructional program. Regardless of whether the teacher had changed his or her teaching style, most felt their students were more self-reliant than "before," that they looked less to the teacher for help, participated in more student-centered discussions, and were more enthusiastic about computer-use lessons than other lessons. Every teacher was of the impression that positive changes were occurring with his or her students because of, or at least alongside of, the students' use of computers.

Summaries of Context and Computer-Use Sessions

The remainder of the forms related to the capturing of information and impressions about the dynamics of the class and teacher as a whole, with and without computer use. As indicated earlier, considerable time and effort went into the coding and interrelating of the school and classroom observations. The final report summarizes these analyses (Collis, 1993, pp. 210–256). As one approach, analyses were done by grouping the classes into "industrialized nations," "East European," and "Third World" categories (with China, Zimbabwe, Mexico, and Costa Rica placed in the latter category). There were predictable differences among these groups in categories such as the types of computers that were available to the classes, but no significant differences were identified on variables relating to student involvement with computers, in student difficulties with computers, or on instructional relevance of computer use. In many respects, the children were similar regardless of part of the world category in which they were placed, such as with their near unanimous interest in computer use or the observation that computer use occurred most often in the context of mathematics or informatics lessons, with geometric topics the most frequent.

However, a wide variety of software programs were being used in the ITEC classrooms. Of all the computer programs used, the programming language LOGO was perhaps the most popular one, accounting for 40% of the total use. The other language used was BASIC (10%). These programming software were mainly used as a tool in mathematics instruction, in some open-ended projects, and to control some external devices. The use of LOGO to enhance the learning of mathematical concepts was quite common in mathematics lessons. For example, in three class-room observations, LOGO was used to teach geometrical concepts (e.g., axial and central symmetry). In other lessons, more open-ended use of LOGO was adopted. For example, in an Informatics class, LOGO was used mainly to help develop children's problem-solving skills and cognitive abilities. The class emphasized a wide variety of applications that fostered interaction and creative practices.

Other than programming, about one quarter of all the videotaped computer lessons used computer-assisted instructional programs (CAI), in the forms of drill and practice and tutorial. They were used in a variety of subject areas such as informatics, language, and again, mathematics (e.g., a drill and practice on subtrac-tion of fractions). More open-ended software programs such as database and graphics programs as well as problem-solving programs were used, accounting for the remaining 25% of the use. In database activities, for example, students were asked to construct a database using information they had collected on a field trip to various beaches. They used key words to categorize information and at a later stage came up with questions to query the database. In one of the problem-solving activities, students were divided into groups of two to three and used a problem-solving program called "Transylvania." In this program, a woman was trapped inside a statue and the objective of the user was to rescue her. To achieve this goal the students had to work out the goal and the strategy and acquire the tools required along the way. Hypercard, graphics, games, and simulation software were also used in several classes.

The Dependent Variable:
Higher Level Cognitive Processing

Clusters of Observable Behaviors. Although context is critical, the core of the ITEC investigations related to children's higher level cognitive development. The preliminary research questions of Phase 1 focused on finding measurable or at least observable indicators of metacognitive activity. The researchers synthesized the comments of the teachers (from Form I), of themselves (from Form J and their other notes), and from the syntheses of the videotapes in order to look for indicators. From the teachers' own words (translated into English), hundreds of comments were extracted (see Collis, 1993, pp. 245–247), and grouped into 11 clusters:

1. Reflection and evaluation of one's own work and of the work of others.
2. Consideration of alternatives.
3. Creativity.
4. Transfer and extrapolation.
5. Seeing new forms of representation.

6. Debugging.
7. Developing strategies for working with others.
8. Showing better performance through better results, better questions, and better work habits.
9. Generating and comparing examples.
10. Planning.
11. Problem solving.

The list of behaviors described by the teachers as being present when their students used computers is impressive, especially when we remember that these teachers were describing in their own words the behaviors they felt they observed in their 9- to 10-year-old students. The list shows a certain amount of convergence, with no pattern of differences in focuses among the different countries and parts of the world. The list also shows again that the domain of interest in ITEC was complex. Something very good was happening in these classrooms when the students used computers, but that something was multifaceted. The teachers perceived it, and were enthusiastic about it, in its various manifestations.

Validation of Clusters. In order to check the researchers' opinions with those of the teachers, completed sets of observation forms and comments sheets (Forms I, J, and K) from 44 videotaped lessons involving 12 of the participating countries and 16 of the classes were analyzed in detail. The researchers identified 10 clusters of indicators of higher level cognitive functioning, and indicated, from the 44 lessons for which complete data were available, the extent to which they perceived the clusters to be observable. Table 4.1 (taken from Lai, 1993) summarizes these conclusions.

Column 5 of Table 4.1 shows that the majority of the researchers observed at least some children displaying indicators of higher level thinking behaviors in the computer-use lessons. In fact, only three indicators of higher level cognitive functioning (comparing similarities and differences, generating new ideas, and recognizing relationships) occurred in less than 60% of the observed lessons. However, the behaviors that were "generally displayed" (Column 4) more than being displayed "just by some students" (Column 3) are much more dispersed, with the highest frequency (42%) being for "Evaluating One's Actions."

Examples of Behaviors Demonstrating Higher Level Cognitive Functioning Skills. A wide variety of examples of higher level cognitive functioning skills were observed by the teachers and researchers in different educational and cultural contexts in this study. To illustrate this, we take problem solving as an example. Most of the videotaped lessons involved some sort of problem-solving activities and various problem-solving skills were displayed. In problem solving, one way to better understand a problem is to relate it to a previous problem, or to one's previous experience. It has been observed in several ITEC classrooms that learners in a computer-based environment were able to relate their own concepts to the programs they were using. For example, in one computer session, when students were

TABLE 4.1

Percentage of Observed Computer-Using Lessons in Which Researchers Saw Various
Indicators of Higher Order Cognitive Functioning (Total Number of Lessons = 44)

Behavior	(1) Observed Lessons in Which the Behavior was Generally not Displayed	(2) Can't Say	(3) Behavior Displayed But Only By Some Students	(4) Behavior was Generally Displayed During the Lesson	(5) Total Observed Lessons (3+4) in Which Behavior was Displayed
	(%)	(%)	(%)	(%)	(%)
1. Relating a problem to previous problems	16	12	32	40	72
2. Formulating appropriate questions	24	0	64	12	76
3. Trying alternative approaches	24	8	36	32	68
4. Evaluating one's actions	21	0	37	42	79
5. Analyzing problems	12	8	44	36	80
6. Recognizing relationships	13	33	29	25	54
7. Generating new ideas	32	28	28	12	40
8. Synthesising information	17	21	33	29	62
9. Observing central issues and problems	20	8	40	32	72
10. Comparing similarities and differences	16	56	12	16	28

engaged in the setting up of a database, they used their personal experiences (i.e., their visit to the beach to see what the tide washed up) to establish key words for database development. In another class it was also observed that some students used their previous experience to help analyze their tasks and figure out what was expected of them.

One efficient way of tackling a problem is to represent it in another way. In several programming situations in this study students were seen using aids to represent their problems. For example, students used notes and diagrams to represent their problems and to do their initial planning before programming in LOGO.

Several researchers have observed that some students had expressed the notion of goal achievement. For example, some students had clearly established their goals of finding or transferring LOGO primitives in their computing activities. In one videotaped lesson, it was observed that students achieved their goal by coordinating the solutions of various subproblems. Initially some students in this class tried to construct one long program. To them, dividing the task into subtasks (problem decomposition) was extra work. But they failed to debug their program and finally came to realize that they should deal with one part of the program at a time (e.g., constructing a picture of a fantastic creature's head instead of the whole creature).

It was clearly seen that the computer lessons provided students with the means to try out alternative approaches to the problems they are supposed to solve. For example, it was observed by a teacher in a database activity that his students did formulate questions and test these questions at the computer. In the follow-up discussion students suggested alternative solutions to problems they had encountered, which often involved reflection on different procedures proposed. Similar observations were reported by other researchers.

The computer-based learning environment sometimes "forces" students in a problem-solving mode and in the process will enhance the learning of problem-solving skills. For example, in one computer session the students were asked to select six words to describe themselves to an alien visitor. In this exercise the students need to analyze what kinds of things described a person and what characteristics made him or her unique as an individual or a culture. They also need to use analysis skills to figure out what was expected of them and reconcile it with their previous experience. They were also using a new computer skill in this activity—combining the paint and draw modes of SuperPaint to create a picture. This activity was a good example of how different higher level thinking skills were exercised in a computer-based learning environment.

"Something Good" is Indeed Happening. Thus, with all these indicators of higher level thinking no singular dependent variable emerged, although the richness and quality of the clusters of behaviors that were validated by the researchers through a variety of synthesis methods are impressive. "Something good" was indeed happening in these computer-use lessons. There did not seem to be a cross-cultural difference in this "something good," in its various manifestations it occurred in many different types of lesson and computer-use situations, but it was not reducible to discrete measurable variables that could be used as a basis for hypothesis testing.

Summary of the Results

Summarizing the results of Phase 1 of the ITEC Project requires nearly 200 pages of comment in the final report (Collis, 1993, pp. 133–320) and sometimes the researchers themselves saw different interpretations of the myriad data and observations and interactions that occurred over the 4 years of the project and the year-long period of school and classroom observations. However, agreement was clear about the conclusions that follow.

Something Good, in Terms of Children's Higher Level Cognitive Development, was Happening in the Computer-Use Classes. A dominant impression from all the data sources was that the computer-use lessons, in their great diversity of forms and attributes, were happy and productive learning situations. Computer-use activities that the teacher and researcher felt had positive cognitive benefits for the children involved were not dependent on particular hardware or software characteristics or classroom environments. Enthusiastic engagement in learning, and presumed higher level cognitive functioning, were taking place where there was only one small classroom computer as well as where there was a lab of networked Macintoshes. Apparently beneficial classroom computer use did not depend on doing a certain type of computer-use activity nor did it need some necessary baseline amount of computer access or some specific type of computer or type of software. In contrast, the way the teacher introduced and organized the computer use was important, the way he or she interacted with the children while the computer use occurred, and the way he or she attempted to reinforce and bring closure and transfer to the computer-use experiences after they were concluded were clearly important. Students interacting with each other, displaying enthusiasm in the way they interact with the learning material, and showing a willingness to sustain this quality of absorption with the learning task over considerable periods of time, also seemed to be common characteristics of the computer use in the classrooms in the ITEC Project. This is ITEC's good news.

Measuring the "Something Good" is Still Difficult. We found encouraging convergence toward visible indicators of presumed higher level cognitive functioning, as teachers and researchers in many different parts of the world came up with the same type of indicators in very different cultural and physical settings. Measurement of higher level cognitive functioning in the realistic social setting of the dynamic classroom, however, remains very difficult to do. Teachers were convinced "good things are going on," the videotapes show the positive characteristics described, but finding a cross-culturally manageable way to validly and reliably measure and document these "good things" did not emerge. Perhaps it is unfair to call this "bad news," but instead challenging news: our convictions about the powerful stimulating effect of classroom computers remain elusive to codify, quantify, and document.

There Seems to Be Only One Contextual Variable Consistently Associated With the Higher Level Cognitive Behaviors: A Good Teacher. Our data from 16 countries and 22 classrooms make it clear that there is no particular rule to follow with respect to computer use for young children. We have seen many different types of lessons, computers, software, school settings, types of student–computer-use patterns—it didn't seem to matter relative to the cognitive indicators that were displayed. But one variable was constant in all our videotapes and observations: a good teacher. What "good" means is another difficult to define concept, and is not characterized by a particular set of behaviors. The ITEC teachers used different teaching strategies, certainly had different personalities and styles of interaction with their students, and used the computers in many different ways. But we, as experienced educators ourselves, recognized quality in these teachers. The ITEC teachers were selected as atypical to begin with, as already using computers with young children in a way that had gained the attention of their peers. We have no way of saying if the computers caused these teachers to be good teachers, but we doubt it. Nor do we have data relating to "ordinary" teachers, those that were not already through their own initiative working with computers.

SUMMARY AND REFLECTIONS

Did We Answer Our Research Questions?

The major research question in ITEC was: "In the context of various combinations of background variables, under what combinations of characteristics of computer use, social interaction surrounding computer use, and instructional integration of computer use is a positive impact on children's higher level cognitive functioning more likely to occur?" How do these sets of conditions vary in different cultures and countries?

Our conclusion to these questions was that given a good teacher, and a teacher willing to be an innovator with computer use, a positive impact on children's higher level cognitive functioning seems to occur. Such a teacher will ensure that the computer use is integrated in an attractive and well-planned learning experience and will interact in close and responsive ways with his or her students as they work with the computers. But these are characteristics of good teaching, not revolutionary insights related to computer use. Thus, optimal combinations of types of computer use, computer software, and ways of using computers did not emerge. The good news about computers may well be that for a good teacher who wishes to innovate with computers and who has the support of the school principal, the computer can be a tool for the development of higher level thinking regardless of the amount of hardware and software available, regardless of the training available to the teacher, regardless of the type of lesson and number of students in the class. This was the ITEC experience.

As for culture-related differences, of course we saw them, but they were most visible in the classroom settings preceding or following computer use. Once the children were at the computers, they almost always were interacting with each other in a task-directed way about the content of the computer-involved activity. Without exception, they appeared engaged in their tasks, enthusiastic about the computer use, not focused on the computer itself but rather, what they were using the computer to do. We saw this sort of quality of absorption in the learning task sustained over considerable periods of time, in all of our classrooms. Thus, these were common characteristics of the ITEC students, again regardless of type of hardware and software, type of computer use, and lesson characteristics, and cultural context. It appeared as if the computer brought a culture of its own that transcended the differences in the natural cultures of the classrooms.

As to the preliminary research questions for ITEC and the expectations of ITEC for its Phase 1 results we found convergence over culture and setting for general types of indicators of higher level cognitive functioning, but not convergence enough to delineate measurable variables that could capture the wealth of different types of quality thinking and metacognitive behavior that was going on. The clusters of behaviors appeared, regardless of country or culture, which is good news for subsequent research.

If we had to suggest a hypothesis for a Phase 2 of ITEC based on the Phase 1 explorations, perhaps it would be to compare the presence of the higher level indicators in classrooms not using computers with those that are, but we already know that any significant differences that would occur could not be accredited to the computer itself, but would be inescapably interrelated with the school, school principal, and the teacher. But this is what we and many others already knew: The effect of computer use on children's higher level cognitive functioning cannot be considered outside of the social and cultural environments affecting the child—his or her community, school, teachers, and school leaders.

What Are the Contributions of ITEC?

However, we do believe that ITEC made major contributions. Extensive pilot testing in the national sites; regular international working meetings in which scientists from the participating countries integrated their ideas and experiences with respect to the impact of computer use in schools into the design and development of the project yielded an observation methodology that has proved to be manageable in an international setting and whose validity has so far been supported. Thus, our expectations as to the development of a protocol usable for classroom observations in a multinational research project have been reasonably satisfied.

More generally, we feel ITEC has made some other general contributions:

- For the field in general, we have documented examples of good practice with computer use in widely varying conditions around the world, that can give encouragement to teachers with vision and enthusiasm regardless of their local conditions.
- We have made the case that there is no "best" or "right" way to use computers with young children, but a myriad of ways, so that fit to local situation can be found.
- We have shown that, within a wide range of types of teacher training, of hardware and software, and of lesson approaches, that children appeared enthusiastic and absorbed in their learning activities, and that good results occurred that transcended the actual content of those activities.
- We saw absolutely no evidence that the 660 ITEC children, regular computer users, were developing any negative social or intellectual characteristics along with their computer use. The children themselves, and their teachers, felt the children were developing more self-reliance, more persistence, and better cooperative skills in problem situations.

And also, although not a contribution of the study for the world in general, the ITEC Project has been valuable for its researchers themselves. We have learned much about each other and each other's countries and approaches to research activity. We have developed a strong network of relationships among ourselves that can still be tapped years after the project has finished. We have watched ourselves function as epistemologists: thinking about our own thinking as we compromised and interpreted and summarized. We have seen among ourselves the phenomena of the computer as a stimulus to reflection and creative thinking, the same sorts of phenomena as we were looking for among the children in the study. As with our ITEC children, we cannot precisely measure the impact of this metacognitive activity in ourselves but we are confident that we have grown from it.

REFERENCES

Clark, R. E. (1985). Confounding in educational computing research. *Journal of Educational Computing Research, 1*(2), 137–148.

Collis, B. A. (1988, July). *Manipulating critical variables: A framework for improving the impact of computers in the school environment.* Paper presented at the EURIT '88 Conference, Lausanne, Switzerland. (ERIC Document Reproduction Service ED 310741)

Collis, B. A. (Ed.). (1993). *The ITEC PROJECT: Information Technology in Education and Children* (Final Report of Phase 1; ED/93/WS/17). Paris: UNESCO, Division of Higher Education.

Cox, M., Rhodes, V., & Hall, J. (1988). The use of computer-assisted learning in primary school: Some factors affecting the uptake. *Computers in Education, 12*(1), 173–178.

Eraut, M., & Hoyles, C. (1988). *Groupwork with computers* (Occasional Paper: InTER/3/88). University of Sussex and London Institute of Education, UK: The Research Consortium.

Feldman, S. C. (1989, March). *An observational study of social processes in microcomputer classrooms.* Paper presented at the annual meeting of the American Educational Research Association, San Francisco.

Fullan, M., Miles, R., & Anderson, R. (1988). *Implementing computers in the school: Lessons from the Ontario experience.* Toronto: Ministry of Education.

Gallimore, R., & Goldenberg, C. N. (1989, March). *School effects on emergent literacy experiences in families of Spanish-speaking children.* Paper presented at the annual meeting of the American Educational Research Association, San Francisco.

Gayeski, D. (1989). Why information technologies fail. *Educational Technology, 29*(2), 9–17.

Hawkins, J., & Sheingold, K. (1986). The beginning of a story: Computers and the organization of learning in classrooms. In J. A. Culbertson & L. L. Cummingham (Eds.), *Microcomputers and education. Eighty-fifth Yearbook of the National Society for the Study of Education* (pp. 40–58). Chicago: University of Chicago Press.

Lai, W. K. (1993). Summary of teachers' and researchers' observations about the appearance of higher-order cognitive functioning. In B. A. Collis (Ed.), *The ITEC PROJECT: Information Technology in Education and Children* (Final Report of Phase 1; ED/93/WS/17). Paris: UNESCO, Division of Higher Education.

Levine, H. G. (1988, April). *Computer-intensive school environments and the reorganization of knowledge and learning.* Paper presented at the annual meeting of the American Educational Research Association, New Orleans.

McGee, G. W. (1987). Social context variables affecting the implementation of microcomputers. *Journal of Educational Computing Research, 3*(2), 189–206.

Metacognition: Thinking about thinking. (1987, Spring). *The Research into Practice Digest,* pp. 13–26.

Newman, D. (1990). Opportunities for research on the organizational impact of school computers. *Educational Researcher, 19*(3), 8–13.

Pea, R. D., & Sheingold, K. (Eds.). (1986). *Mirrors of minds: Patterns of experience in educational computers.* Norwood, NJ: Ablex.

Peled, Z. (1993). Observations and protocols on children and classroom behavior. In B. A. Collis (Ed.), *The ITEC PROJECT: Information Technology in Education and Children* (Final Report of Phase 1; ED/93/WS/17). Paris: UNESCO, Division of Higher Education.

Peled, E., Peled, Z., & Alexander, G. (1989). Project Comptown: Educational intervention and action research. *British Journal of Educational Technology, 20*(2), 84–105.

Perkins, D. N., & Salomon, G. (1989). Are cognitive skills context bound? *Educational Researcher, 18*(1), 16–25.

Perret-Clermont, A. N., & Schubauer-Leoni, M. L. (Eds.). (1989). Social factors in learning and instruction. Special Issue, *International Journal of Educational Research, 13*(6), 575–580.

Phi Delta Kappa. (1987). High road, low road, end of the line for CAI and programming. *The Kappan, 86*(7), 547–548.

Salomon, G. (1990, April). *What is so special about computer-mediated communication? Studying the flute and the orchestra.* Paper presented at the annual meeting of the American Educational Research Association, Boston.

Schoenfeld, A. H. (1989). Ideas in the air: Speculations on small-group learning, environmental and cultural influences on cognition and epistemology. *International Journal of Educational Research, 13*(1), 1–119.

Tharp, R. (1989, March). *The institution and social context of teaching.* Paper presented at the annual meeting of the American Educational Research Association, San Francisco.

Tikhomirov, O. K. (1988). Vygotsky's theory as a methodological basis for a cross-cultural Study on the impact of IT in education on child psychological development. In B. A. Collis (Ed.), *The ITEC Project Information Technology in Education and Children* (Final Report of Phase 1; pp. 8–13). Paris: UNESCO, Division of Higher Education.

Vygotsky, L. S. (1986). *Thought and language.* Cambridge, MA: MIT Press. (Original work published 1966)

Vygotsky, L. S. (1978). *Mind in society: The development of higher psychological processes.* Cambridge, MA: Harvard University Press.

Wertsch, J. V. (1985). *Vygotsky and the social formation of mind.* Cambridge, MA: Harvard University Press.

Zimmerman, B. J., Smith, C. P., Bastone, L., & Friend, R. (1989, March). *Social processes in microcomputer learning: A social cognitive view.* Paper presented at the annual meeting of the American Educational Research Association, San Francisco.

Chapter 5

Information Technology
From the Child's Perspective

Gerald A. Knezek
Keiko T. Miyashita
Takashi Sakamoto

This chapter is based on findings from the Young Children's Computer Inventory Project (YCCI), which ran from 1990 to 1994 and examined the psychological impact of computer use on children in Grades 1 through 4. An overview of the project was provided in chapter 2.

This chapter begins with a brief description of how young children perceive computers, then provides a description of the subjects and methodology of the overall project. A detailed explanation of the 19 major findings are included next, followed by a discussion of insights gained from the project findings.

INFORMATION TECHNOLOGY
THROUGH THE EYES OF A CHILD

Several computer programs have been designed to help young children develop creativity, cognitive skills, and other basic skills such as reading, writing, and mathematics (Bracey, 1984; Genishi, McCollum, & Strand, 1985; Johnson, 1985; Yawkey, 1986). However, few research studies had been conducted to investigate how young children judge or view IT.

When young children use computers, they may feel that the computers are their playmates and also new toys for them. Genishi, McCollum, and Strand (1985) observed six kindergarten children using the program LOGO for 3 months. A variety of social interactions (child-to-child, child-to-computer, and child-to-adult) were observed by the researchers. They recorded a significant amount of interaction between children, and between children and adults. The interaction between children and the computer was also recorded. While programming, children often spoke to the computers calling their computers "you" or "he" instead of "it." While interacting with computers, young children may feel that the computers are their playmates.

Computers may also be just new toys for young children. Before the YCCI project was started, the researchers conducted a pilot study. Fourteen kindergarten and first-grade children were allowed to freely interact with a computer and 5 CAI-type software packages at home for about 3 months. There was significant reduction in the time students spent with computers over the 3 months of the project. The children may have initially viewed the computer as a "new toy," which eventually sits in the corner with other "old toys."

Young children have much curiosity and desire to explore new things. Although many adults have some fear of using computers, most young children can enjoy using (playing with) computers. In our study, both U.S. and Japanese first- to third-grade students who used computers reported enjoying computers more than did the students not using computers. Moreover, the computer enjoyment feeling tended to remain high or increase as the children grew older (Miyashita, Knezek, & Sakamoto, 1993).

Young children may simply enjoy using computers without any fear. In our study, in 1993, first- through eighth-grade students at one United States public school completed YCCI questionnaires. The data was factor analyzed and the factor "computer anxiety" emerged if data included children older than the fourth grade. However, for students in Grades 1 to 4, there was no separate "computer anxiety" factor—anxiety items were simply placed at the opposite extreme of computer enjoyment. Although many interpretations are possible for this finding, one plausible explanation is that when young children are in the "state" of enjoying computers, they have none of the residual anxiety complexes that often plague adults. Perhaps for children, something that is fun, by definition, cannot also produce anxiety.

Many interesting issues related to children and IT remain unanswered at the time of this writing. The sections that follow focus on questions that have been answered, at least in part, by the YCCI Project.

YCCI SAMPLE AND METHODOLOGY

As shown in Fig. 5.1 to 5.3, the YCCI Project surveyed students in Grades 1 to 4 in three areas of Japan, two regions of the United States, and two areas of Mexico. Twenty-six schools supplied 5,517 Likert-type questionnaire returns from students over the 4 years of the project.

YCCI research activities began with a pilot test in 1990 involving one public school in Tokyo, one public school in Texas, and one weekend school for children of Japanese families stationed in the United States. The project expanded to 14 school sites in Japan and the United States in 1991, and further expanded to 21 school sites in Japan, Mexico, and the United States in 1992. For 1993, research

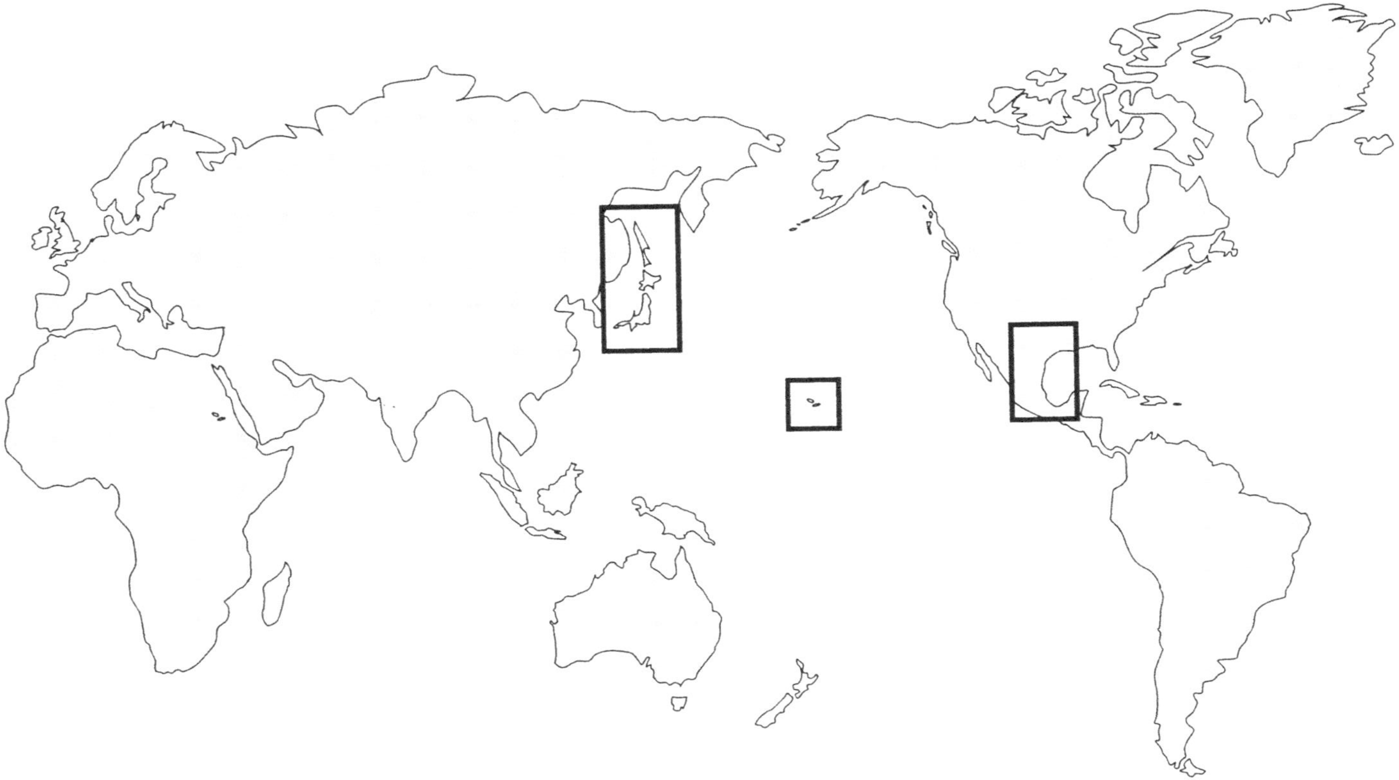

FIG. 5.1.   YCCI sites (Japan, Mexico, and the United States).

71

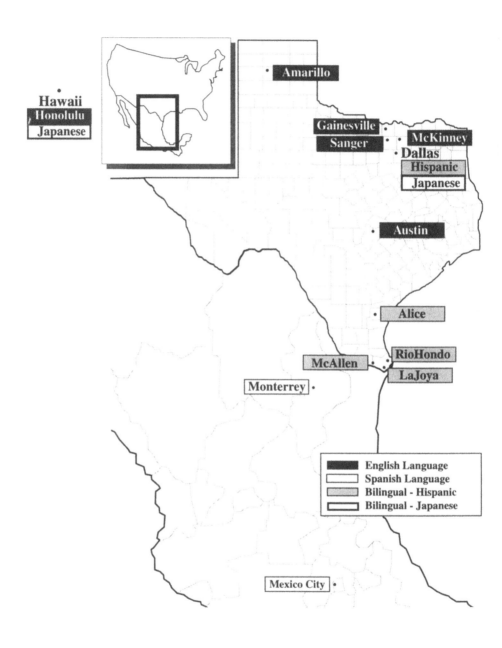

FIG. 5.2.   YCCI sites (the United States and Mexico).

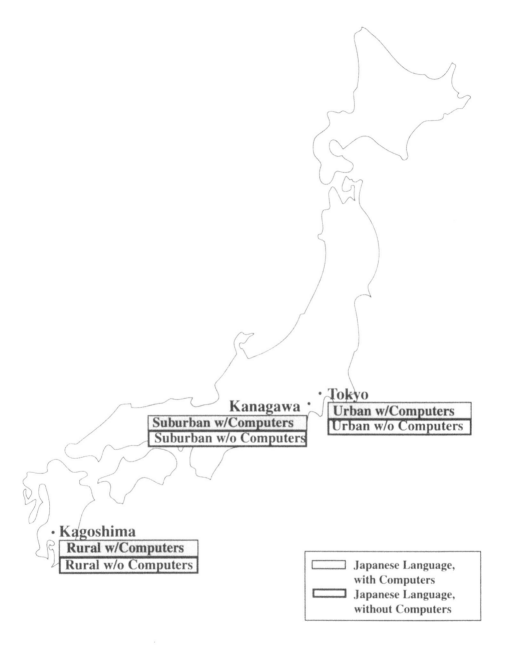

Kanagawa ·
Suburban w/Computers
Suburban w/o Computers

· Tokyo
Urban w/Computers
Urban w/o Computers

· Kagoshima
Rural w/Computers
Rural w/o Computers

Japanese Language,
with Computers
Japanese Language,
without Computers

FIG. 5.3.   YCCI sites (Japan).

activities were refocused on follow-up questions and the number of sites was reduced to 8 in Japan and the United States.

Sampling Rationale

Seven different schools with and without computers were used to gather data in Japan. The six 1991 and 1992 schools were selected from three geographically distinct areas: urban, suburban, and rural. In each area, two public schools were selected: one school with microcomputers and one school without microcomputers (Knezek & Miyashita, 1991; Miyashita, 1994). Two weekend schools for Japanese children whose families were residing in the United States, also provided data for the study in Japanese.

This sampling procedure was selected for two primary reasons: (a) to be able to determine if the effects of introducing computers in schools were location specific or universal throughout Japan (i.e., if the effect was the same in all three areas, one could be reasonably confident that the effect was true for all of Japan); and (b) to determine if the learning-related dispositions of Japanese students living in foreign nations greatly differed from Japanese students residing in their home geographic locale and culture.

In the United States, nine separate schools gathered English-language data. For 1991 and 1992, data were also provided from a rural public school plus one urban and one suburban public school (Knezek & Miyashita, 1993b). These were selected to match the comparable schools in Japan, thereby providing a time-synchronized basis for comparing trends among computer-using students in the United States to those in Japan. Data were also gathered via the Spanish-language version of the YCCI from five bilingual-Hispanic elementary school programs in Texas during 1992 (one of these continued to provide data in 1993). Most of these schools were located in the Rio Grande Valley area of Texas, near Mexico (Knezek, Miyashita, & Sakamoto, 1994). This provided a time-synchronized basis for comparing the dispositions of recent Hispanic immigrants to the United States to those of their native Spanish-speaking peers in Mexico, and their native English-speaking peers in the United States.

Two elementary schools in Mexico provided data via the Spanish-language version of the YCCI during 1992. The locations of these schools were Monterrey and Mexico City (Knezek, Miyashita, & Sakamoto, 1994). One school followed the standard United States curriculum and provided the majority of instruction in English, while the other followed the traditional curriculum for Mexico and instructed in Spanish, thus offering an opportunity to contrast the effects of school environment and culture versus geographic location.

Research Design

The research design for the YCCI Project was initially envisioned (in 1990) to be quantitative, pseudo-experimental, single-treatment, pretest–posttest (Campbell & Stanley, 1963). The major treatment and control groups were to be paired schools in urban, suburban, and rural areas of Japan—one school selected in each pair was using computers and the other not. United States sites, and later, Mexico sites as well, were scheduled to serve as additional, cross-cultural controls. The initial two-country approach was consistent with Brislin's (1983) contention that "If research hypotheses are supported in studies with very different populations, the findings can be taken more seriously than those hypotheses supported only in studies of homogeneous populations within one country" (p. 371). The decision to add Mexico as a new research initiative for 1992 was in keeping with Foschi's (1980) judgment that an explanatory model produced from cross-cultural research can be considered robust if it is supported in at least three cultures.

This basic design was preserved for the duration of the project, but many additional hypotheses were "tested" using multivariate data analysis techniques such as cross-lagged regression analysis, cluster analysis, and disriminant function analysis. Scaling methods (Dunn-Rankin, 1983) were employed as well, as were ethnographic research techniques such as examination of videotape footage, interviews, and on-site observation. Thus two kinds of findings emerged from the YCCI Project. The first, which can be considered "hard" findings, are those based on the initial research design and well-established statistical techniques. The second, which could be called "soft" findings, are based on exploratory data analysis and qualitative research techniques.

In summary, from a historical perspective, the YCCI Project can be considered opportunistic research. The project was made possible by Japan's decision not to introduce large numbers of computers into the educational environment during the 1980s, while scholars and policymakers contemplated the consequences, followed by its decision to carry out large-scale introduction of computers in the early 1990s (Knezek, Miyashita, & Sakamoto, 1990; see Fig. 5.4). This made it possible to answer "before-versus-after" questions that had become difficult, if not impossible to answer in the United States.

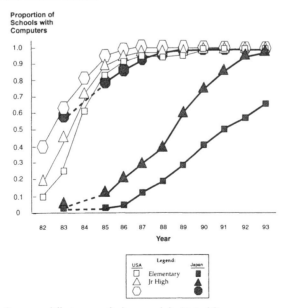

FIG. 5.4.   Computer diffusion rates for Japan and the United States.

Description of Instrument

The YCCI questionnaire, a 48-item Likert-type survey instrument, was developed to carry out this research (Knezek & Miyashita, 1993a; Miyashita & Knezek, 1992). The six psychological constructs it measures can be informally described by the meanings commonly associated with the terms in standard English (Urdang, 1968; Zeleny, 1990):

Computer Importance: perceived value or significance of knowing how to use computers.

Computer Enjoyment: amount of pleasure derived from using computers.

Study Habits: mode of pursuing academic exercises within and outside class.

Empathy: a caring identification with the thoughts or feelings of others.

Motivation/Persistence: unceasing effort; perseverance; never giving up.

Creative Tendencies: inclinations toward exploring the unknown, taking individual initiative, finding unique solutions.

Each construct is formally defined, for operational purposes, by the items summed to form a Likert-type measurement index. YCCI items are listed in Table 5.1.

Reliability and Validity

During 1990–1991, an iterative procedure involving double back-translation, content validation, pilot testing, construct (factor) validation, and reliability verification was used to produce the 48-item Likert-type questionnaire from an initial pool of 155 potential items (Miyashita & Knezek, 1992). Because YCCI construction began with items translated from Japanese to English, and then back to Japanese, and because 1991 and 1992 survey administrations took place in March to April to correspond with the end of the Japanese school year, it is believed this research is not particularly prone to the "Western bias" that is commonly found in cross-cultural research (Hulin, 1987). The overall internal consistency reliability of the scale is .92, utilizing 44 of the 48 items contained in the instrument (Knezek & Miyashita, 1993b; see Table 5.2). Subscale reliabilities range from a low of .66 to a high of .85 when data from all language/culture administrations is combined. These reliabilities fall within the range of "minimally acceptable" (.65–.70) to "very good" (.80–.90), according to the guidelines provided by DeVellis (1991) regarding acceptable reliabilities for research instrument scales.

Subjects

Table 5.3 shows that 5,517 student responses from 46 school administrations were included in the study. Many of the same schools provided data for 3 or 4 consecutive years, so the actual number of unique subjects was much smaller than the 5,517 questionnaire returns. Approximately 3,000 students completed surveys one or more times during the 4 years of the project. The data for the 46 school administrations was gathered from 26 separate schools.

TABLE 5.1

YCCI Items Ordered by Strength of Contribution to Subscale

Computer Importance
9   I can learn many things when I use a computer.
12 I believe that it is very important for me to learn how to use a computer.
8   I know that computers give me opportunities to learn many new things.
3   I will be able to get a good job if I learn how to use a computer.
11 I believe the more often teachers use computers, the more I will enjoy school.
6   I would work harder if I could use computers more often.
10 I enjoy lessons on the computer.

Computer Enjoyment
1   I enjoy doing jobs which use a computer.
2* I am tired of using the computer.
10 I enjoy lessons on the computer.
5   I enjoy computer games very much.
4   I concentrate on a computer when I use one.

Motivation/Persistence
16 If I do not understand a problem, I will not stop working on it.
22 I think about many ways to solve a difficult problem and I never give up.
23 I never forget to do my homework.
21 I enjoy working on a difficult problem.
17 When I don't understand something, I keep working until I find the answer.
15 I study by myself without anyone forcing me to study.

Study Habits
24 I like to work out problems which I can use in my life every day.
18 I review my lessons every day.
19 I try to finish whatever I begin.
20 Sometimes, I change my study habits.
15 I study by myself without anyone forcing me to study.
25 If I do not understand my teacher, I ask him/her questions.

Empathy
30 I worry when I see a sad friend.
26 I feel sad when I see a child crying.
29 I feel sad when I see old people alone.
27 I sometimes cry when I see a sad play or movie.
35 I feel happy when I see a friend smiling.
28 I get angry when I see a friend who is treated badly.
31 I feel very happy when I listen to a song I like.
32 I do not like to see a child play alone, without a friend.
33 I feel sad when I see an animal hurt.

Creative Tendencies
42 I find different kinds of materials when the ones I have do not work.
40 I create many unique things.
44 I make a plan before I start to solve a problem.
36 I examine unusual things.
39 I tend to consider various ways of thinking.
37 I find new things to play with or to study, without any help.
43 I examine unknown issues to try to understand them.
38 When I think of a new thing, I apply what I have learned before.
46 I invent new methods when one way does not work.
41 I do things by myself without depending on others.
45 I invent games and play them with friends.
47 I choose my own way without imitating methods of others.
48 I tend to think about the future.

* Reversed Item

TABLE 5.2
Internal Consistency Reliability for YCCI English, Japanese, and Spanish Versions
Based on 1992 Data (Grades 1–3)

	Items	Overall	English	Japanese	Spanish
Creative tendencies	13	.85(.82)	.83	.83	.79
Computer enjoyment	5	.72(.70)	.66	.77	.57
Computer importance	9	.77(.76)	.69	.77	.70
Empathy	9	.77(.76)	.74	.79	.61
Study habits	6	.80(.76)	.60	.70	.55
Motivation/persistence	6	.66(.64)	.65	.74	.34
Overall	44	.92(.90)	.90	.89	.86

TABLE 5.3
YCCI Schools and Subjects by Type

	Grade Level	Japan Schools	Japanese in U.S.	U.S. Schools	Hispanic in U.S.	Mexico Schools	Total Schools (Subjects)
1990	1–2	1 (99)	1 (51)	1 (112)	—	—	3 (262)
1991	1–2	6 (734)	—	8 (707)	—	—	14 (1,441)
1992	1–3	6 (1,236)	1 (59)	7 (1,072)	5 (247)	2 (422)	21 (3,036)
1993	1–4	2 (200)	2 (251)	3 (266)	1 (61)	—	8 (778)
Total		15 (2,269)	4 (361)	19 (2,157)	6 (308)	2 (422)	46 (5,517)

Procedure

All questionnaires at the Japan sites and the U.S. schools for Japanese dependents were completed by the children, with their parents, at home, in Japanese. For English and Spanish administrations in the United States, questionnaires were completed during school time, under teacher supervision, at all sites in 1990, 1991, and 1992. For 1993, the two public schools administered questionnaires in school, while a private school sent questionnaires home to be completed under parental supervision. Mexico administrations were completed during school time, under teacher supervision, in Spanish.

Rates for completion of usable questionnaires in Japanese varied from approximately 50% to 99%, by school, with all public schools in Japan returning greater than 90%. For the United States and Mexico, the completion rate resulting from school administration is estimated to be at least 90% of the potential student sample. Typically all students not absent on the day of administration completed questionnaires, and typically all teachers in a given grade agreed to have their students complete questionnaires.

CHRONOLOGY OF RESULTS

1990 Results

For the pilot-test year of the study, major findings were: (a) U.S. computer-using first and second-grade students in Texas were more positive than Japanese-in-Japan noncomputer-using students on their attitudes toward computers; (b) U.S. students were less empathetic than their Japanese counterparts; (c) U.S. students were more positive on study habits; and (d) no significant differences were found in the areas of motivation/persistence or creative tendencies. An additional finding was that Texas-based Japanese students typically fell between the Japanese-in-Japan students and the traditional Texas students on the attributes measured (Knezek & Miyashita, 1991).

1991 Results

Major findings for the first full-scale research year were: (a) Japanese first- and second-grade children who used computers tended to like computers more than children who did not use computers; (b) there was no evidence that computer use had a negative impact on children's empathy; and (c) there was no strong evidence that 1 or 2 years of computer use in school had a positive impact on children's motivation/persistence, study habits, or creative tendencies. An additional finding was that any of several different types of computer experiences (CAI alone, mixed CAI and LOGO programming, mixed word processing and graphics production) could produce a positive effect on children's attitudes toward computers. Results for 1991 also reconfirmed the homogenous nature of the public education environment in Japan. There were no significant differences among urban, suburban, and rural children's scores for any of the areas measured (Miyashita, 1991, 1994; Miyashita et al., 1993).

1992 Results

The second full-scale research year focused on longitudinal trends in the data among first, second-, and third-grade students in Japan, Mexico, and the United States. Computer access was found to raise computer enjoyment and perceived computer importance. Computer access was not found to lower empathy. No strong ($p < .01$) influence was found on motivation/persistence, study habits, or creative tendencies, and gender differences emerged only for empathy (females were more empathetic). Students' prevailing psychological tendencies (their dispositions) were generally quite positive in the four noncomputing areas measured, and dispositions among all students tended to decline from the first through the third grades in school. However, no novelty effect, which is the tendency for ratings to decline with increasing age or over time, was found for computer enjoyment. An unanticipated outcome was that bilingual Hispanic students in the United States frequently reported dispositions more positive than either the students in Mexico or the native English-speaking students in the United States. Differential item response characteristics for Japan and the United States led to caution in drawing additional conclusions from direct comparisons among average responses for the three nations (Knezek & Miyashita, 1993b; Knezek, Miyashita, & Sakamoto, 1993).

1993 Results

For the third research year, the study was refocused to address several specific follow-up questions. Six schools representing a cross-section of the 21 sites used in the previous year were retained, and two new schools in Hawaii were added to the group. All schools in the sample provided data from Grades 1 to 4. Major findings were: (a) reconfirmation that computer exposure has a positive impact on computer enjoyment and computer importance; (b) confirmation that computer exposure can have a positive ($p < .01$) impact on study habits and motivation/persistence (when students with 4 years of computer exposure are included); (c) confirmation that Japanese students living in Japan, Hawaii, and Texas have similar dispositions regardless of residence, as do native English-speaking students in Texas and Hawaii; and (d) new probable causal relations in the direction of higher creative tendencies leading to higher perceived computer importance, greater computer enjoyment leading to higher perceived computer importance, and greater empathy leading to higher motivation/persistence (Knezek, Lai, & Southworth, 1994; Knezek, Miyashita, & Sakamoto, 1994, 1995).

MAJOR FINDINGS BY CATEGORY

In this section, the major findings of the project are presented according to issue or area of relevance, and aggregated across all 4 years of the study. Explanatory information including tables and graphical displays are provided to supplement the narrative. Comparisons and contrasts with work by other researchers in the field are also provided for selected topics.

Children's Questionnaires

1. Young children in Grades 1 to 3 have stable ($r = .90$) psychological dispositions that can be measured by self-report inventories.

When our project began, we were not certain whether it would be possible to obtain reliable opinions from children as young as age 6. Our experience has been that it is possible. Once young children understand the question, they are very enthusiastic about providing an opinion, and quite certain about their choice of options. This outcome has made all the other findings possible.

Psychological Impact of Computer Exposure

2. Early initial computer exposure (Grade 1) in school increases computer enjoyment by approximately two thirds of a standard deviation.
3. Early computer exposure in school increases perceived computer importance by approximately one half standard deviation.

Early exposure of 40 minutes or more per week in school boosted perceived Computer Importance and Computer Enjoyment to a point where 8 to 12 years (based upon regression slopes) would be expected to elapse before the attitudes of computer users again match those of non-computer users. (Knezek et al., 1993, p. 196)

Previous studies have indicated that computer access can improve attitudes toward computers for students of high school and college ages (D'Souza, 1988; Justen, Adams, & Waldrop, 1988). A Soviet–U.S. study of 8- to 12-year-old children also supported this claim (Martin, Heller, & Mahmoud, 1992). Our findings support the hypothesis that young children with computer experience in school will tend to have higher attitudes toward computers than young children without computer experience in school.

Students in Japan who used computers, students in the United States who used computers, and students in Mexico who used computers, all rated the computer as higher in enjoyment and importance than did Japanese students who did not use computers (Miyashita et al., 1993). Results are shown graphically in Fig. 5.5 and 5.6.

These findings are based primarily on a comparison of Japanese computer-using to noncomputer-using students. The findings are consistent across 1991, 1992, and 1993 data (Knezek, Miyashita, & Sakamoto, 1994; Miyashita, 1991, 1994; Miyashita et al., 1993;). For example, effect sizes (standardized mean differences for treatment groups; Kulik, 1994) for computer enjoyment in Japan were .52, .67, and .85 for 1991, 1992, and 1993, respectively; the effect sizes for computer importance were .52, .41, and .52 for the same years (Knezek, Miyashita, & Sakamoto, 1994, p. 26).

Effects Due to Time/Maturation

4. Early computer exposure (up to 4 years) in school does not appear to have a negative effect on empathy.
5. Early computer exposure (up to 4 years) in school does not appear to have a positive effect on creative tendencies.
6. Three or 4 years of computer exposure in primary school can have a measurable positive impact on motivation and study habits.

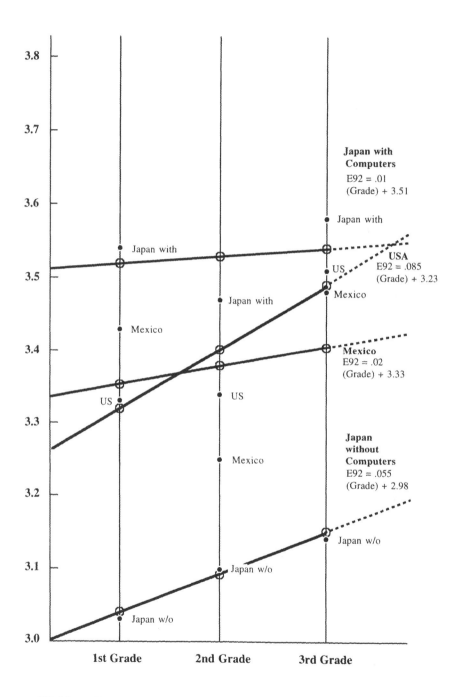

FIG. 5.5.   1992 mean ratings for computer enjoyment.

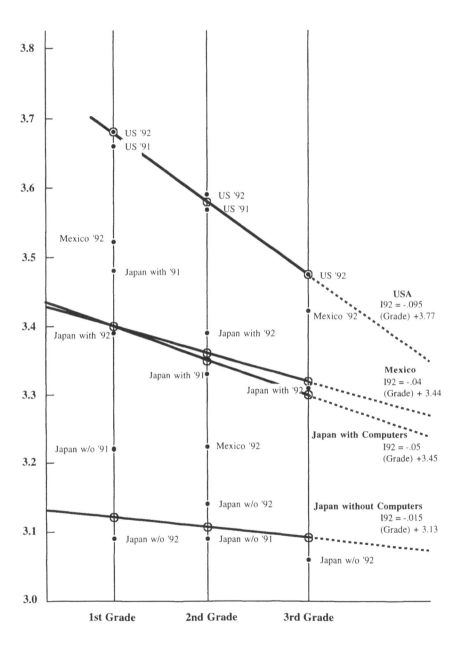

FIG. 5.6.   1991 and 1992 mean ratings for computer importance.

83

early computer exposure in school does not appear to lower student empathy, as the National Council on Educational Reform in Japan (1986, 1987) once feared might take place. (Knezek et al., 1993, p. 198)

The U.S. Software Publishers Association gathered evidence to support the claim that microcomputers have the power to "motivate students and to improve their attitudes about learning and themselves" (Bialo & Sivin, 1990). Studies by Clements and others (Clements 1987, 1991; Clements & Nastasi, 1988) have shown that LOGO programming experiences can foster higher order thinking and certain forms of creativity in children. A study including 762 children in Grades 4 to 6 in Japan (T. Sakamoto, Zhao, & Sakamoto, 1991) found that a combination of word processing at home and programming in school was associated with higher self-reported creativity, but a more recent study (A. Sakamoto & Sakamoto, 1993) indicated that the causation is probably in the direction of creativity leading to increased computer use.

Our analyses of student scores on motivation/persistence, creative tendencies, empathy, and study habits showed no consistent differences between Japanese students using computers, versus those not using computers, in the 1991 or 1992 data (Miyashita et al., 1993). However, analysis of the 1993 Japanese data confirmed that computer exposure can have a positive impact on computer enjoyment [$F(1, 191) = 41.7, p < .00005$], computer importance [$F(1, 195) = 13.7, p < .0004$], study habits [$F(1, 184) = 8.24, p < .005$], and motivation/persistence [$F(1, 184) = 6.73, p < .01$] (Knezek, Miyashita, & Sakamoto, 1994). The positive findings for study habits and motivation/persistence were new for the 1993 survey, which also contained data for fourth-grade students (with 4 years of computer exposure) for the first time. The emergence of significant findings for learning dispositions only during the fourth year of the project, lends additional support to the concept that at least 3 or 4 years of exposure to computers in school is necessary before a measurable positive impact on study habits and motivation/persistence takes place.

Effects Due to Time/Maturation

7. Children's self-reported values on motivation, study habits, empathy, and creative tendencies tend to decline as they progress from Grades 1 to 3.
8. There appears to be a weak tendency for this decline to take place with regard to computer importance (novelty effect).
9. This decline does not normally take place with regard to computer enjoyment, which tends to remain high or increase as the children grow older.

the fact that Computer Importance does not decline (regress) as much as many other dispositions measured, and that Computer Enjoyment does not regress at all, may be due in part to the "chameleon effect" of computers. As universal machines, through changes in software and activities, computers have the capability to grow with children. (Knezek et al., 1993, p. 200)

In Wilder, Mackie, and Cooper's (1985) study involving 1,600 kindergarden through Grade 12 students in the United States, "The most striking finding with respect to attitudes toward the computer was one of decreased liking by all students (with increased age)" (p. 218). This phenomenon has come to be known as the *novelty effect*. It was also confirmed for 339 Grade 4 through 10 students in the United States, "using longitudinal data from a large, representative sample to study the evolution of responses to computers over an extended period of time" (Krendl & Broihier, 1992, p. 217). Unfortunately, our findings do not generally concur with those of previous researchers regarding the novelty effect and attitudes toward computers.

Computer Enjoyment.   Computer enjoyment trends appear to run the opposite direction anticipated for a novelty effect. Computer enjoyment either remains very high among computer-using students or continues to rise across Grades 1 to 3 (see Fig. 5.5). This is true for Japan, Mexico, and the United States. Even among Japanese students who have never used computers in school, the trend over 1 year, by grade, is toward stable or increased computer enjoyment with age.

Computer Importance.   There appears to be a weak novelty effect in this area. Figure 5.6 illustrates that, among Japan students, Mexico students, and United States students who have used computers, 1992 third-grade ratings of computer importance tended to be lower than second-grade student ratings, and both of these groups tended to rate computer importance lower than first grade students. Yet computer importance for 1992 second-grade students, viewed as a class by nation, did not significantly ($p < .01$) decline from 1 year earlier, when they were first-grade students. Neither was there a significant decline for the 1992 third-grade students in Japan or the United States. In addition, there was no significant decline in computer importance or computer enjoyment for 89 third-grade students at one Texas public school whose responses were paired with their own questionnaire responses from 1 year earlier (Miyashita et al., 1993).

Novelty Effect for Schooling.   The tentative conclusion drawn from many results is that the novelty effect applies to several of the constructs parents and educators might hope would remain high or increase during school years, as well as to some kinds of attitudes toward computers. As illustrated in Fig. 5.7, the general trend for all four noncomputing constructs in Japan, Mexico, and the United States was down, as student ages/grade levels increased.

It seems possible that both kinds of attitudes toward computers (enjoyment and importance) tend to run counter to the novelty effect, as some research with older students and adults shows, but that computer importance is not strong enough to overcome the general trend toward less positive dispositions among older primary school students on almost all psychological dispositions we measured. As illustrated in Fig. 5.7, absolute ratings for all noncomputing dispositions except study habits in Japan were quite tightly clustered. If one overlays Fig. 5.7 with Fig. 5.5 and 5.6, then the attitudes toward computers of the students without school computer

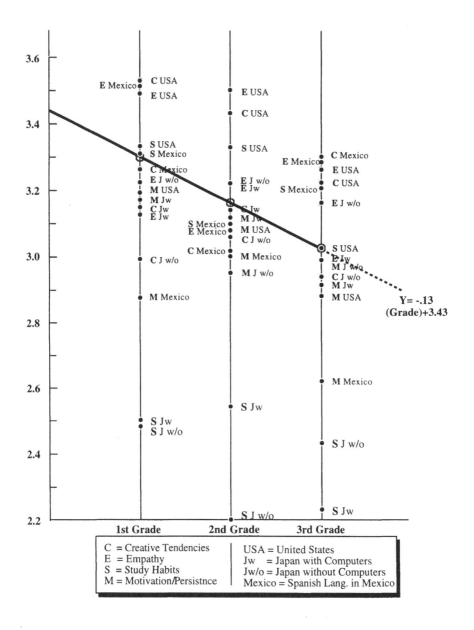

FIG. 5.7. 1992 mean item ratings on four learner disposition subscales.

access fall at the very bottom of the student dispositions cluster, whereas attitudes toward computers of students with computer access lie at the top. This is generally true across the age ranges studied, which implies an effect independent of age. Additional evidence is presented in the discussion of causal relations to support the hypothesized positive impact of computer exposure on computer enjoyment and computer importance, independent of age.

Effect of Length of Exposure. Two participating Japanese schools did not use computers during 1991, but began using computers in 1992. This provided an opportunity to test the effect of different lengths of exposure on attitudes toward computers. The six Japanese schools were divided into three groups: Group 1, which contained one school, had no computers during 1991 or 1992; Group 2, which contained two schools, had no computers during 1991 but had been using computers for 3 months by the time the questionnaire was administered in 1992; and Group 3, which contained three schools, used computers during 1991 as well as during 1992.

Findings were that the Japanese students using computers for less than 1 year and the students using computers for more than 1 year both scored significantly higher ($p < .01$) on the two subscales than the group not using computers. However, the students using computers for less than 1 year were not significantly different from the group using computers more than 1 year, on either subscale. The group with no computer exposure was different from the other two, but the group with 1 year of exposure or less was not significantly different from the group with more than 1 year of exposure, at any grade level.

These outcomes reconfirmed that computer use in school leads to higher perceptions of computer importance and higher levels of computer enjoyment. They failed to support the hypothesis that additional exposure to computers over time leads to lower ratings of computer importance and computer enjoyment.

Age Versus Length of Exposure. These findings are generally consistent with a 1993 examination of the relative contributions of age versus computer exposure to trends in psychological dispositions for 178 students in Grades 1 through 5 attending a Saturday-only Japanese advancement school in Hawaii (Knezek, Lai, & Southworth, 1994). Three results of the Hawaii study pertinent to the current topic were: (a) all six standardized partial regression coefficients for each of the YCCI subscales, predicted as a function of age, were negative—that is, all measured dispositions went down as age (and grade level) increased; (b) age explained a significant portion of the decline in computer importance, while time since first computer exposure was a positive contributor to computer importance; and (c) time since first computer exposure was a positive contributor to motivation, after removing the effect of age (NS). The first result is consistent with the trends shown for 1992 data from Japan, Mexico, and the United States in Fig. 5.6. The first and second results together imply that declining dispositions are primarily the result of increasing age and/or schooling, rather than increased computer exposure.

Findings from Japan and Hawaii are also generally consistent with a 1993 path analysis on data from a Texas public school that indicated that increased age probably leads to lower creative tendencies and lower study habits, but not to decreased computer enjoyment, computer importance, or motivation (see Knezek, Miyashita, Sakamoto, & Sakamoto, 1994, for details).

Implications of Findings.   Apparently, the kinds of attitudes toward computers measured by the YCCI questionnaire do not go down because of increased computer use. Students in Japan with 3 months of exposure had roughly the same attitudes toward computers as did their peers of the same age with 1 year plus 3 months of exposure. Among students in Hawaii, increased exposure to computers was a positive contributor to computer attitudes, after controlling for age. Time-lag correlations among Texas students showed increased age to be a negative contributor to study habits and creative tendencies, but not computer importance or computer enjoyment.

Ratings for computer importance among students without computer access in school remain fairly constant throughout Grades 1 through 3. Students who use computers in school tend to have a higher perception of the computer's importance than do students not using computers in school; however, among primary school students with computer access, older students tend to perceive the computer as less important than their younger counterparts. Results to date do not support the hypothesis that this decline is caused by increased exposure to computers. Rather, findings indicate that the decline is probably due to increased maturation and/or age.

Computer enjoyment remains high or possibly even increases during the first 3 years of school. Exposure in school seems to give a large boost to a student's rating of computer enjoyment, so that for several years it will be higher than that of a student not using computers in school. However, even primary school students with no school access to computers tend to have higher ratings on computer enjoyment if they are older. This implies that factors outside of school, such as home use of computers, may have a strong influence on a student's degree of computer enjoyment. By contrast, increased computer importance seems to be instilled largely through the schools.

10. Effects 1 through 5 and 7 through 9 are robust across several different types of computer applications (robustness unknown for Effect 6).

children's attitudes toward computers were improved by any of several different types of computer experiences. (Miyashita, 1994, p. 78)

The most common type of computer use in primary schools in the United States has historically been drill and practice (Becker, 1990), but the trend is toward more tool type applications such as word processing, databases, or simulations (Martin, Heller, & Mahmoud, 1992). Guidelines developed by the National Association for the Development of Young Children in 1991 encourage open-ended tools and tutee-mode applications such as LOGO programming to enhance children's development and creative potentials (Clements, Nastasi, & Swaminathan, 1993).

In our study, computer applications spanned a wide range from drill and practice, tutorials, and educational games in computer laboratories, to free-form story composition and graphics production in laboratories and classrooms, to group participation in single-computer story construction in a classroom. No particular form was restricted to any country. However, there was a tendency toward guided, uniform-participation whole-group or small-group activities in Japan and Mexico, whereas individual student or small-group activities dominated in the United States.

The 1991 Japan population of our study, in which three schools were each matched with comparable schools not using computers, confirmed that any of several different kinds of educationally relevant computer experiences can improve attitudes toward computers: CAI at the urban site ($p < .005$), LOGO programming plus CAI at the suburban site ($p < .001$), and word processing plus graphics production at the rural site ($p < .001$) (Miyashita, 1991). These findings are consistent with those of a U.S.–Soviet study reported by Martin et al. (1992) that "most of the children thought that whatever they were doing on the computer was fun" (p. 182).

11. Effects 7 through 9 are not necessarily true for children emigrating to a new (foreign) culture.

The Hispanic Immigrant Anomaly

Bilingual Hispanic students in the U.S. maintain (and in some cases increase) their initially high learning-related dispositions from grades 1–3. This trend is contrary to the novelty effect found to be common among English-speaking students in America, Japanese-speaking students in Japan, and Spanish-speaking students in Mexico. (Knezek, & Miyashita, 1993b, p. 18)

The expectation for bilingual-Hispanic students in the United States was that their psychological dispositions would generally lie in between those of students in Mexico and those in the United States. Instead, bilingual Hispanics as a group were higher ($p < .01$) than all other groups on computer importance and study habits. Four of the six dispositions measured (computer importance, computer enjoyment, creative tendencies, and empathy) had positive regression slopes for Grades 1 through 3, and slopes for the other two were practically flat (-.04 and -.08). Among bilingual-Hispanic students, the trend was for dispositions that were high at Grade 1 to remain high. Dispositions with room to increase tended to do so as students progressed to higher grade levels.

Discussion. A sizable portion of the bilingual Hispanic students in our study were from families who recently immigrated to the United States. Duran and Weffer (1992), in their review of the literature, pointed out that recent United States immigrants from Mexico "are in a certain sense a select group" (p. 167), better educated than their Mexican counterparts, and economically and technologically different from earlier agricultural immigrants (Portes, 1979; Portes, McCleod, & Parker 1978). According to Duran and Weffer, Matute-Bianchi (1986) found that students recently migrated from Mexico valued education and hard work similar to Japanese Americans. "Mexican immigrant students stressed a goal-directed approach to education and had a stronger achievement level and graduation rate than American-born students" (Duran & Weffer, 1992, p. 167). Duran and Weffer themselves found that successful Hispanic high school students who were immigrants attributed their success to family encouragement and their willingness to work hard in school. Parents of these students believed that education was not an end in itself, but "the means to better jobs and higher income" (Duran &Weffer, 1992, p. 179).

Effects Due to Gender

12. No gender differences were found for computer importance, computer enjoyment, motivation, study habits, or creative tendencies at the first-grade level, and no consistent differences by gender were found at the second- and third-grade level.
13. Females were more empathetic than males at the first-, second-, and third-grade levels.
14. Effects 12 through 13 are true for English-speaking United States students in Texas, native-language Japanese students in Japan, and Spanish-speaking natives in Mexico.

A meta-analysis by Kay (1992) of 98 studies found unequal attitudes toward computers by gender, in favor of males. Studies have often found higher attitudes toward computers among males in junior high, high school, and college (Collis, 1985; Collis & Williams, 1987; Wilder, Mackie, & Cooper, 1985). Elementary school results are more mixed. Wilder et al. found that in a New Jersey school district, "Boys like computers and video games more than girls do, from kindergarten through high school" (p. 220). They also explained that "the differences between the sexes in attitudes toward the computer are statistically significant, but quite small in an absolute sense" (p. 221). Martin et al. (1992) found no significant gender differences in attitudes toward computers for 8- to 12-year-old children in the United States and the Soviet Union.

We found no strong ($p < .01$) gender differences among computer users in their attitudes toward computers at the first-grade level, and no consistent differences at the second or third-grade level (Knezek & Miyashita, 1993b). This is true for the United States, Japan, and Mexico. We also found no consistent gender differences in motivation, study habits, or creative tendencies. These findings are especially convincing in light of the strong evidence for consistent gender differences in empathy, which we define as a caring identification with the thoughts or feelings of others. Females appear to be more empathetic, even at this early age, in all three nations. These findings are graphically displayed in Fig. 5.8.

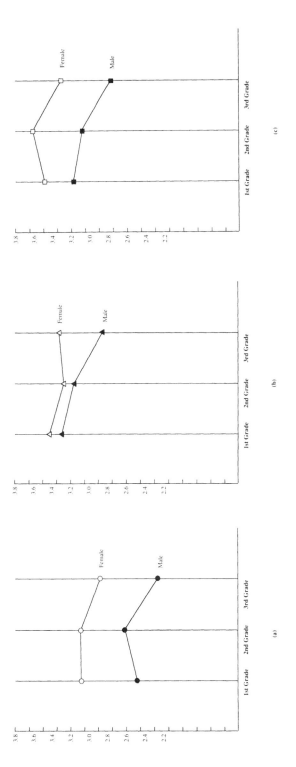

FIG. 5.8.   1992 mean ratings by gender for empathy in (a) Japan, (b) mexico, and (c) the United States.

One recent analysis of YCCI data verified that gender differences in dispositions other than empathy may begin to emerge among older elementary school students (Knezek, Lai, & Southworth, 1994). As part of a study of 178 students in Grades 1 through 5 attending a Saturday-only school for dependents of Japanese nationals living in Hawaii, males and females were compared on each of the six YCCI subscales. Results were that females reported a greater degree of empathy than males, as anticipated, and females were also higher in motivation/persistence than their male counterparts. No significant differences by gender were found on the other four subscales. These findings imply that new gender differences may develop on attributes measured, as the subjects mature. Lack of significant gender differences in YCCI subjects' attitudes toward computers do not necessarily conflict with research showing strong gender differences at higher grade levels.

Directionality of Selected Effects

15. Increased computer enjoyment appears to lead to higher ratings on computer importance.
16. Higher creative tendencies appear to lead to higher computer importance.

Educators in many parts of the world believe that appropriate computer activities can improve children's psychological dispositions (prevailing attitudes) related to learning, which will eventually lead to improved cognitive performance (Collis, 1993; Pelgrum & Plomp, 1993). However, research to determine the effects of computer use on creativity has produced mixed results (Bruce, 1989; Clements, 1991; A. Sakamoto & Sakamoto, 1993), as has research regarding the effect of computer use on motivation for learning (Krendl & Lieberman, 1988; Lepper, 1985; A. Sakamoto, Hatano, & Sakamoto, 1992).

During 1993, the authors attempted to formulate a probable causal model among nine computer use, learning disposition, and background variables gathered from subjects over consecutive years, in two nations (Knezek, Miyashita, & Sakamoto, 1994). The attributes involved were age, gender, computer exposure, motivation, study habits, empathy, creative tendencies, computer importance, and computer enjoyment. Two regression analysis techniques were employed. Both were aimed at producing path coefficients that show probable directions of influence among the variables included in the model.

Findings From 1993 Japan Data. Figure 5.9 contains significant ($p < .01$) path coefficients derived from regression analyses performed on responses from 198 Japanese students in Grades 1 through 4 at two urban public elementary schools in Tokyo in 1993. Four independent regression analyses, for example: computer importance $= F$(computer exposure), were carried out. The resulting standardized regression coefficients (betas) are written above the probability values on the lines indicating direction of influence in Fig. 5.9. The strongest relationship ($\beta = .42$) is for computer enjoyment, whereas the weakest ($\beta = .17$) are for both study habits and motivation/persistence. Complete findings were:

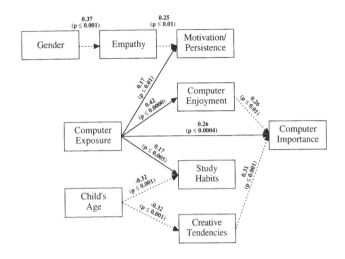

FIG. 5.9. Combined causal model: computer exposure and psychological dispositions.

1. Computer exposure leads to greater computer enjoyment (ß = .42, $p < .00005$).
2. Computer exposure leads to greater perceived computer importance (β = .26, $p < .0004$).
3. Computer exposure leads to greater motivation/persistence (ß = .17, $p < .01$).
4. Computer exposure leads to improved study habits (ß = .17, $p < .01$).

Findings From Paired 1991–1992 U.S. Data.   A cross-lagged model (Markus, 1979) was applied to paired data from one United States school in order to further explore these relationships. Regression equations similar to those used for the 1991, 1992, and 1993 Japan data were constructed for the paired 1991–1992 data gathered from the United States school. The major change was that time-lag regression models were constructed to attempt to determine the directional influences of psychological dispositions on each other. For example, in order to determine if creative tendencies influenced computer importance, or if higher computer importance led to greater creative tendencies, the outcomes of two models were contrasted: 1992 computer importance = F(1991 computer importance, 1991 creative tendencies, gender, age) versus 1992 creative tendencies = F(1991 creative tendencies, 1991 computer importance, gender, age).

As shown in Fig. 5.9, the result was a significant path (β = .31, $p < .001$) in the direction of higher creative tendencies leading to higher perceived computer importance. The influence in the opposite direction was not significant. Fifteen pairs of this type of regression equation were produced, one set for each of six psychological dispositions paired with the other five. The significant findings from this analysis were as follows:

1. Higher creative tendencies appear to positively influence perceived computer importance (β = .31, $p < .001$)

2. Greater computer enjoyment appears to lead to higher perceived computer importance ($\beta = .26$, $p < .01$)
3. Greater empathy appears to lead to higher motivation/persistence ($\beta = .25$, $p < .01$)
4. Being female leads to higher empathy ($\beta = .37$, $p < .001$)
5. Increased age leads to lower creative tendencies ($\beta = -.32$, $p < .001$)
6. Increased age leads to less positive study habits ($\beta = -.32$, $p < .001$).

Discussion. The analysis of the data from Japan reconfirms the positive impact of 1 year or more of computer exposure on computer enjoyment and computer importance. It also lends additional support to the concept that at least 3 or 4 years of exposure to computers in school, at the typical rate, is necessary before a measurable positive impact on study habits and motivation/persistence takes place. In addition, it reaffirms the negligible impact of gender and age on these relations. Taken all together, these results imply that positive benefits of computer exposure accrue to both males and females, and that the effect may not differ for students of different ages (within the age parameters of Grades 1–4).

The time-lag analysis of data from the U.S. school reaffirms that children tend to lower their self-reported creative tendencies and self-reported study habits as they advance from Grade 1 to Grade 3 in school. It also reaffirms that females are more empathetic than males. New findings are that higher empathy leads to higher motivation/persistence, higher computer enjoyment leads to higher perceived computer importance, and higher creative tendencies lead to more positive ratings of computer importance (which in turn can lead to greater use; Coovert, Salas, & Ramakrishna, 1992). The latter finding is consistent with similar research recently completed in Japan (A. Sakamoto & Sakamoto, 1993), and calls into question the belief that computer use increases creativity.

The composite model shown in Fig. 5.9 is less valid than either of its halves, because each half is based on findings from two separate groups in different countries. Nevertheless, there are no contradictions between the two halves of the model, and the combination forms a single, holistic basis for formulating and testing future hypotheses.

Influence of Culture

17. The effect of early computer exposure in school on computer enjoyment appears to be largely universal, culture-free.
18. Computer importance appears to be influenced by both exposure and culture.
19. Study habits appear to be strongly influenced by culture.

For 1993, six schools representing a cross-section of the 21 sites used in the previous year were retained, and two schools in Hawaii were added (see Table 5.4). Six one-way analysis of variance procedures were run for each of the YCCI subscales, using all eight sites. The overall F was significant ($p < .01$) for every subscale, so Scheffe's multiple-range tests for post hoc comparisons between all pairs of sites

TABLE 5.4

Descriptive Statistics for 1993 Survey Sites (Grades 1–4)

School	Type	Subjects	Form
101	U.S. (Texas) public with computers	143	English
104	U.S. (Texas) private with computers	99	English
109	U.S. (Hawaii) pseudopublic with comp.	24	English
201	U.S.-Japanese advancement in Texas	96	Japanese
202	U.S.-Japanese advancement in Hawaii	155	Japanese
304	Japanese public with computers	105	Japanese
305	Japanese public without computers	95	Japanese
604	U.S. bilingual Hispanic with computers	61	Spanish

were used to determine precisely which sites were distinctive on any given subscale (Knezek, Miyashita, & Sakamoto, 1994). Knowledge of significant selected contrasts, in combination with visual examinations of the site clusterings in Fig. 5.10, was used to develop the following conjectures about the influences of culture and computer use on each of the six dispositions.

1. *Computer Enjoyment*. Increased computer enjoyment seems to be a simple function of meaningful computer exposure. This does not appear to be confounded by culture. This trend is illustrated by the two clear clusters of sites (for computer use vs. nonuse) found in the category of computer enjoyment on Fig. 5.10.

2. *Computer Importance*. The effect of computer exposure on computer importance does not appear to be identical to the effect on enjoyment. More positive ratings of computer importance seem to be largely a function of computer exposure, but they are also influenced by culture. These trends are illustrated by the three clusters (for U.S. students with computers vs. Japanese students with computers vs. Japanese students without computers) shown in the category of Computer Importance on Fig. 5.10.

3. *Empathy*. Ratings for empathy seem to be a simple function of Western versus Eastern culture, independent of computer experience. This is shown by the two very tight clusters for empathy in Fig. 5.10, where Japanese students with computers and without computers are in the same cluster.

4. *Study Habits*. Study Habits appear to be strongly influenced by Western versus Eastern culture. There are very large separations in Fig. 5.10 of the kind described for empathy. However, there is much more variation within clusters for study habits, compared to empathy, so other effects besides culture may be present. A causal path from computer exposure to study habits found in the 1993 YCCI data indicates that computer exposure is one of the factors, in addition to culture, that can influence study habits in a positive manner.

5. *Motivation/Persistence*. This disposition does not appear to be a simple function of either computer use or culture. Perhaps other factors not examined in this study are the primary determinants of motivation. As with study habits, findings from

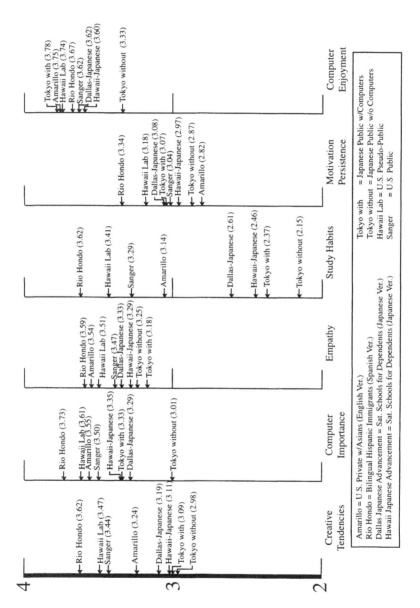

FIG. 5.10. Combined ratings: United States versus Japan with computers versus Japan without computers (1993).

Amarillo = U.S. Private w/Asians (English Ver.)
Rio Hondo = Bilingual Hispanic Immigrants (Spanish Ver.)
Dallas Japanese Advancement = Sat. Schools for Dependents (Japanese Ver.)
Hawaii Japanese Advancement = Sat. Schools for Dependents (Japanese Ver.)

Tokyo with = Japanese Public w/Computers
Tokyo without = Japanese Public w/o Computers
Hawaii Lab = U.S. Pseudo-Public
Sanger = U.S Public

Creative Tendencies

Rio Hondo (3.62)
Hawaii Lab (3.47)
Sanger (3.44)
Amarillo (3.24)
Dallas-Japanese (3.19)
Hawaii-Japanese (3.11)
Tokyo with (3.09)
Tokyo without (2.98)

Computer Importance

Rio Hondo (3.73)
Hawaii Lab (3.61)
Amarillo (3.55)
Sanger (3.50)
Hawaii-Japanese (3.35)
Tokyo with (3.33)
Dallas-Japanese (3.29)
Tokyo without (3.01)

Empathy

Rio Hondo (3.59)
Amarillo (3.54)
Hawaii Lab (3.51)
Sanger (3.47)
Dallas-Japanese (3.33)
Hawaii-Japanese (3.29)
Tokyo without (3.25)
Tokyo with (3.18)

Study Habits

Rio Hondo (3.62)
Hawaii Lab (3.41)
Sanger (3.29)
Amarillo (3.14)
Dallas-Japanese (2.61)
Hawaii-Japanese (2.46)
Tokyo with (2.37)
Tokyo without (2.15)

Motivation Persistence

Rio Hondo (3.34)
Hawaii Lab (3.18)
Dallas-Japanese (3.08)
Tokyo with (3.07)
Sanger (3.04)
Hawaii-Japanese (2.97)
Tokyo without (2.87)
Amarillo (2.82)

Computer Enjoyment

Tokyo with (3.78)
Amarillo (3.75)
Hawaii Lab (3.74)
Rio Hondo (3.67)
Sanger (3.62)
Dallas-Japanese (3.62)
Hawaii-Japanese (3.60)
Tokyo without (3.33)

4
3
2

1993 YCCI data indicate that computer exposure in school, over several years, can have a significant positive impact on motivation/persistence.

6. *Creative Tendencies.* Ratings for creative tendencies appear to divide along Western versus Eastern cultural lines, rather than according to extent of computer use. One interesting anomaly for this category is that of the Texas private school with computers (104), which lies in the "Eastern" cluster rather than the "Western" cluster. It is hypothesized that this may be due to the significant numbers of children of Asian immigrant families who are attending this school system.

ADDITIONAL OBSERVATIONS REGARDING CULTURE

Site Clusters. A cluster analysis of the mean values for all sites was carried out to further explore the similarities and differences among the 1993 sites. As shown in Fig. 5.11B, the first two sites to merge in the reduction from the initial eight clusters to seven were Sites 201 and 202, the Texas and Hawaii Japanese advancement schools. Site 109, the English-speaking Hawaii school, merged with the mainland U.S. public school, Site 101, at the next step. Although the two Hawaii schools had adjoining campus locations, they did not merge until the last step, when all eight sites were combined into a single cluster. Apparently these two sites are "sister schools" only with respect to proximity.

Influence of Culture. Based on the dendogram shown in Fig. 5.11C, several observations can be made about the impact of school environment (including location and programs) versus culture on the psychological dispositions measured by the YCCI. All four United States sites merged with each other before combining with the Japanese cluster. On the Japanese side, the first two sites to merge were the Japanese advancement schools, even though they were far apart geographically. These sites next combined with the Japan public school using computers, and were eventually joined by the Japan public school not using computers.

Effect of Computer Use. The differing pattern for some Japanese sites probably represents differences due to computer use, because a previous analysis (Miyashita, 1994) gave strong evidence of initial homogeneity among the Japanese schools, and because almost all students attending the Saturday-only Japanese advancement schools use computers in their Monday through Friday schools in the United States. Furthermore, the strong correlation ($r = .69$) found at the Hawaii Japanese advancement school between time in the United States and time since first computer use corroborates evidence from Japan (Knezek, Miyashita, & Sakamoto, 1990; Watanabe & Sawada, 1990) that most elementary students in Japan prior to 1990 did not have access to computers in school. The conclusion is that most Japanese advancement school students received their exposure to computers after coming to the United States, although not in advancement school, and that exposure made their attitudes toward computers similar to those of computer-using students in Japan.

A. Agglomeration Schedule using Average Linkage (Between Groups)

Stage	Clusters Combined Cluster 1	Cluster 2	Coefficient	Stage Cluster 1st Appears Cluster 1	Cluster 2	Next Stage
1	4	5	.046600	0	0	3
2	1	3	.063000	0	0	4
3	4	6	.090400	1	0	6
4	1	2	.197600	2	0	5
5	1	8	.368500	4	0	7
6	4	7	.397367	3	0	7
7	1	4	1.461650	5	6	0

B. Cluster Membership of Cases using Average Linkage (Between Groups)

Number of Clusters

Label	Case	7	6	5	4	3	2	
101	1	1	1	1	1	1	1	1 (Mainland U.S. Public)
104	2	2	2	2	2	1	1	1 (Mainland U.S. Private w/Asians)
109	3	3	3	1	1	1	1	1 (Hawaii U.S. Pseudo-Public)
201	4	4	4	3	3	2	2	2 (Mainland U.S. Japanese Advancement)
202	5	5	4	3	3	2	2	2 (Hawaii Japanese Advancement)
304	6	6	5	4	3	2	2	2 (Japanese Public w/Computers)
305	7	7	6	5	4	3	3	2 (Japanese Public w/o Computers)
604	8	8	7	6	5	4	1	1 (Mainland U.S.Bilingual Hispanic)

C. Dendrogram using Average Linkage (Between Groups)

Rescaled Distance Cluster Combine

```
C A S E        0        5       10      15      20      25
Label  Seq     + ------- + ------- + ------- + ------- + ------- +

201    4       ┐
202    5       ├─┐
304    6       ┘ │
305    7       ──┤
101    1       ┐ │
109    3       ┤ │
104    2       ┘ │
604    8       ──┘
```

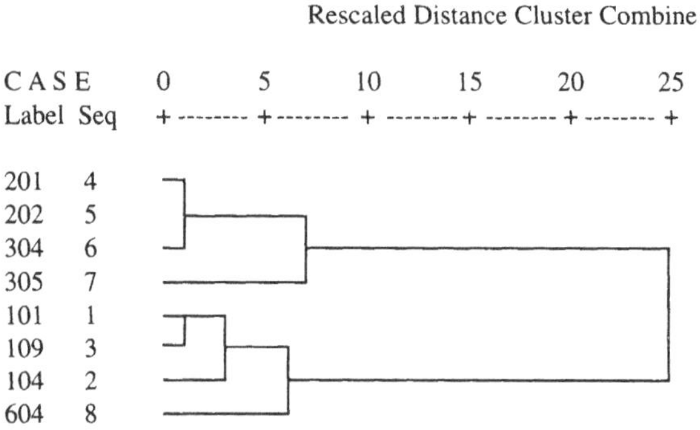

FIG. 5.11.   Cluster analysis for eight 1993 school sites.

98

Homogeneity Within Nations.   One overriding conclusion to be drawn from the cluster analysis is that Japanese children, whether or not they have been using computers, are still culturally Japanese and distinct from Americans. The large jump in the error coefficient (.4 to 1.5) from Stage 6 to Stage 7 in Fig. 5.11A indicates the linkages within clusters are much better when the United States and Japanese students are kept separate, as in Stage 6, rather than combined as in Stage 7.

Strong Native Culture.   One purpose for adding the Hawaii schools in 1993 was to address the question of how comparable is data gathered from Japanese dependents in Hawaii to data gathered from Japanese dependents attending school on the U.S. mainland (Knezek, Lai, & Southworth, 1994). As previously reported, six one-way analysis of variance procedures were run for each of the YCCI subscales using all eight 1993 sites. Although the overall F was significant for every subscale, Scheffe's multiple-range test for pairs of sites failed to confirm any difference ($p <$ .01) between the Texas Japanese advancement school (201) and the Hawaii Japanese advancement school (202) on any of the six subscales measured (Knezek, Lai, & Southworth, 1994). These findings support the contention that Japanese children living abroad are members of a fairly homogeneous group regardless of where they are temporarily located in the United States. The latter conclusion is also consistent with the findings reported by Miyashita (1994) regarding homogeneity of Japanese-in-Japan students regardless of urban, suburban, or rural location, on the attributes measured by the YCCI.

Additional confirmation for these results is provided by the graphic representations in Fig. 5.10 of the mean scores for eight sites on the six psychological dispositions measured by the YCCI. The response profiles for the Texas Japanese Advancement School (201) and the Hawaii Japanese Advancement School (202) are very similar to each other, as are the profiles for the Texas and Hawaii public schools (101 and 109).

There is also evidence that United States culture may remain strong among United States-affiliated children residing in Mexico. A cluster analysis for 1992 data showed that students attending an American-curriculum school in Monterrey, Mexico, had dispositions similar to public school students in Texas and unlike their peers in Mexico City. Apparently the Monterrey students retained many of the values of their United States parent(s), even though they were fluent in Spanish and typically born and raised in Mexico.

DISCUSSION AND INSIGHTS

Findings from the Japan data indicate that any of several types of educationally relevant computing activities in school can result in positive attitudes toward computers on the part of students in Grades 1 through 3. The increase is rapid, definitely occurring within the first year of computing access for one hour or more per week, and probably within the first several months. In addition, there is little decline is this positive attitude up through Grade 3, if meaningful computer exposure is continued. (We do not know what happens if computer access is removed.) These findings seem to render unnecessary the current discussions in the literature over which type of computer application is best for young children. If the goal is positive attitudes toward computers, then it seems that many forms will suffice.

Our findings, taken as a whole, are not definitive on the issue of which type of application is most appropriate for primary school children, if positive outcomes regarding learning dispositions are the goal. On the one hand, data from Japan indicates that children who receive up to 3 years of computing experiences including CAI, LOGO programming, and process writing with a word processor, can indeed have measurably higher self-reported values on motivation and study habits than their peers who have been without computers in school for the same 1 to 3 years. Furthermore, children from the final year "treatment" (computer-using) school, who had 1 to 2 years of computing when surveyed a year earlier, were not significantly different from the other two Japan computer-using schools, on any of the six psychological dispositions measured. This implies that the other two Japan treatment schools, with different mixes of computer applications, may also have shown positive effects of computer exposure on motivation and study habits if we had continued to gather data from them through the third year.

On the other hand, data from Texas, where all students surveyed had some exposure to computers, seems to indicate that different types of computing environments can be associated with differences in self-reported attitudes toward computers, motivation, and creative tendencies. For 1991, the Texas public school which consistently employed an exploratory, discovery learning approach to computer utilization was found to be significantly higher ($p < .01$) than several other schools in the areas of motivation and creative tendencies (Knezek, Miyashita, Jones, & Bills, 1992). The trend was similar for 1992 data from the same school (School 107)—motivation, creative tendencies, and study habits were all high ($p < .01$). In addition, in the 1992 data, the school which consistently employed integrated learning systems for primary school computing activities (School 102) was signficantly lower ($p < .01$) than several other schools on computer enjoyment and creative tendencies.

It is easy to assume that these differences were all due to "the computer," but our research design was not structured to enable us to determine the direction of causality. Visits to many of the schools, interviews with students and teachers, and examination of video footage has led to the conclusion that the school environment, rather than the type of software utilized, is probably the major factor responsible for the kinds of differences reported in the previous paragraph. It appears that external factors, such as the type of neighborhood and the extent of family support for schooling, sometimes drag a school down to the point where even the best principals and teachers cannot lift it up. If a primary school falls at the balance point, then a good principal seems to be able to lift it up. Then, in turn, good teachers can work their pedagogical magic, and computers can be a part of it.

Quantitative data from one YCCI school in the United States, and data gathered by other researchers in Japan, seem to be consistent with the scenario described in the previous paragraph. Time-series data analysis indicates that creative children probably perceive computers as important to their schooling and hence seek to use them more, rather than vice-versa. In addition, the trends-by-grade-level shown for motivation and study habits earlier in this chapter (see Fig. 5.7) imply that the significant positive effect of computer use on these dispositions may be that it keeps them from declining as rapidly as normal, over time, rather than causing them to rise.

Data gathered from children in three nations over a span of 4 years does not indicate that the impact of computer use in a school environment is restricted to or strongly influenced by any particular culture. On the contrary, the psychological impacts of computer exposure appear to be surprisingly similar across the three cultures we have examined. Nevertheless, these findings should not be taken as a recommendation to disregard the local culture when implementing computers in schools. Certainly many aspects of schooling are strongly influenced by culture, and so also can we expect for the computer to be, as it is integrated into the existing educational environment.

REFERENCES

Becker, H. J. (1990). How computers are used in United States schools: Basic data from the 1989 I.E.A. Computers in Education Survey. *Journal of Educational Computing Research, 7,* 385–406.

Bialo, E., & Sivin, J. (1990). *Report on the effectiveness of microcomputers in schools.* Washington, DC: Software Publishers Association.

Bracey, G. W. (1984). Computers and readiness. *Phi Delta Kappan, 68,* 243–244.

Brislin, R. (1983). Cross-cultural research in psychology. *Annual Review of Psychology, 34,* 363–400.

Bruce, R. (1989). Creativity and instructional technology: Great potential imperfectly studied. *Contemporary Educational Psychology, 14,* 241–256.

Campbell, D. T., & Stanley, J. C. (1963). *Experimental and quasi-experimental designs for research.* Chicago: Rand McNally.

Clements, D. H. (1987). Longitudinal study of the effects of logo programming on cognitive abilities and achievement. *Journal of Educational Computing Research, 3,* 73–94.

Clements, D. H. (1991). Enhancement of creativity in computer environments. *American Educational Research Journal, 28*(1), 173–187.

Clements, D. H., & Nastasi, B. K. (1988). Social cognitive interactions in educational computer environments. *American Educational Research Journal, 25,* 87–106.

Clements, D. H., Nastasi, B. K., & Swaminathan, S. (1993). Young children and computers: Crossroads and directions from research. *Young Children, 48*(2), 56–64.

Collis, B. (1985). Psychosocial implications of sex differences in attitudes toward computers: Results of a survey. *International Journal of Women's Studies, 8*(3), 207–213.

Collis, B. A. (Ed.). (1993). *The ITEC Project: Information technology in education and children* (Final report of phase 1; ED/93/WS/17). Paris: UNESCO, Division of Higher Education.

Collis, B. A., & Williams, R. L. (1987). Cross-cultural comparison of gender differences in adolescents' attitudes toward computers and selected school subjects. *The Journal of Educational Research, 81*(1), 17–27.

Coovert, M. D., Salas, E., & Ramakrishna, K. (1992). The role of individual and system characteristics in computerized training systems. *Computers in Human Behavior, 8*(4), 335–352.

DeVellis, R. F. (1991). *Scale development: Theory and applications.* Newbury Park, CA: Sage.

D'Souza, P. V. (1988). A CAI approach to teaching an office technology course. *Journal of Educational Technology Systems, 17*(2), 135–140.

Dunn-Rankin, P. (1983). *Scaling methods.* Hillsdale, NJ: Lawrence Erlbaum Associates.

Duran, B., & Weffer, R. (1992). Immigrant's aspirations, high school process, and academic outcomes. *American Educational Research Journal, 29*(1), 163–181.

Foschi, M. (1980). Theory, experimentation, and cross-cultural comparisons in social psychology. *Canadian Journal of Sociology, 5*, 91–102.

Genishi, C., McCollum, P., & Strand, E. (1985). Research currents: The interactional richness of children's computer use. *Language Art, 62*(5), 526–533.

Hulin, C. L. (1987). A psychometric theory of evaluations of item and scale translations. *Journal of Cross-Cultural Psychology, 18*(2), 115–142.

Johnson, J. F. (1985). Characteristics of preschoolers interested in microcomputers. *Journal of Educational Research, 78*(5), 299–305.

Justen, J. E., III, Adams, T. M., II, & Waldrop, P. B. (1988). Effects of small group versus individual computer-assisted instruction on student achievement. *Educational Technology*, 50–52.

Kay, R. H. (1992). Understanding gender differences in computer attitudes, aptitudes, and use: An invitation to build theory. *Journal of Research on Computing in Education, 25*(2), 159–171.

Knezek, G., Lai, M., & Southworth, J. (1994). Psychological dispositions of children residing in Hawaii in the context of a multinational study on computing. In G. Knezek (Ed.), *Studies on children and computers: The 1993–94 Fulbright series* (pp. 39–60). Denton: Texas Center for Educational Technology.

Knezek, G., & Miyashita, K. (1991). Computer-related attitudes of primary school students in Japan and the United States. *Educational Technology Research* (Japan), *14*, 17–23.

Knezek, G., & Miyashita, K. (1993a). *Handbook for the Young Children's Computer Inventory*. Denton: Texas Center for Educational Technology.

Knezek, G., & Miyashita, K. (1993b). *Learner dispositions related to primary school computing in three nations: 1992 results*. Paper presented to the American Educational Research Association Conference, Atlanta, GA.

Knezek, G., Miyashita, K., Jones, G., & Bills, A. (1992, January) *Learner attitudes among primary school computer users: 1991 Texas survey results* (Tech. Rep. No. 92.1). Denton: Texas Center for Educational Technology.

Knezek, G., Miyashita, K., Sakamoto, T., & Sakamoto, A. (1994). Causal relations among YCCI attributes. In G. A. Knezek (Ed.), *Studies on children and computers: The 1993–94 Fulbright series* (pp. 29–38). Denton: Texas Center for Educational Technology.

Knezek, G., Miyashita, K., & Sakamoto, T. (1990). Computers in education: Japan vs. the United States. In A. McDougall & C. Dowling (Eds.), *Computers in education* (pp. 775–780). North-Holland: Elsevier Science.

Knezek, G., Miyashita, K., & Sakamoto, T. (1993). Cross-cultural similarities in attitudes toward computers and the implications for teacher education. *Journal of Information Technology for Teacher Education, 2*(2), 193–204.

Knezek, G. A., Miyashita, K. T., & Sakamoto, T. (1994). *Young Children's Computer Inventory Final Report*. Denton: Texas Center for Educational Technology.

Knezek, G. A., Miyashita, K. T., & Sakamoto, T. (1995). Findings from the Young Children's Computer Inventory Project. In J. D. Tinsley & T. J. van Weert (Eds.), *World Conference on Computers in Education VI* (pp. 909–920). London: Chapman & Hall.

Krendl, K. A., & Broihier, M. (1992). Student responses to computers: A longitudinal study. *Journal of Educational Computing Research, 8*(2), 215–227.

Krendl, K. A., & Lieberman, D. A. (1988). Computers and learning: A review of recent research. *Journal of Educational Computing Research, 4*, 367–389.

Kulik, J.A. (1994). Meta-analytic studies of findings on computer-based instruction. In E. L. Baker & H. F. O'Neil, Jr. (Eds.), *Technology assessment in education and training* (pp. 9–33). Hillsdale, NJ: Lawrence Erlbaum Associates.

Lepper, M. R. (1985). Microcomputers in education: Motivational and social issues. *American Psychologist, 40*, 1–18.

Markus, G. B. (1979). *Analyzing panel data*. Beverly Hills, CA: Sage.

Martin, D., Heller, R., & Mahmoud, E. (1992). American and Soviet children's attitudes toward computers. *Journal of Educational Computing Research, 8*(2), 155–185.

Matute-Bianchi, M. E. (1986). Ethnic differences and patterns of school success and failure among Mexican-descent and Japanese-American students in a California high school: An ethnographic analysis. *American Journal of Education*, 95, 233–255.

Miyashita, K. (1991, December). *Influence of computer use on attitudes toward computers, motivation to study, empathy, and creativity among Japanese first- and second-grade children*. Unpublished doctoral dissertation, University of North Texas, Denton, TX.

Miyashita, K. (1994). Effect of computer use on attitudes among Japanese first-and second-grade children. *Journal of Computing in Childhood Education*, 5(1), 73–82.

Miyashita, K., & Knezek, G. (1992). The Young Children's Computer Inventory: A Likert Scale for assessing attitudes related to computers in instruction. *Journal of Computing in Childhood Education*, 3(1), 63–72.

Miyashita, K., Knezek, G., & Sakamoto, T. (1993). Changes in learning dispositions among students using computers during the first three years of school. In A. Knierzinger & M. Moser (Eds.), *Informatics and changes in learning* (Vol. 2, pp. 701–703). Gmunden, Austria: Institute for School & New Technology.

National Council on Educational Reform. (1986, April 23). *Summary of second report on educational reform*. Tokyo: Government of Japan.

National Council on Educational Reform. (1987, April 1). *Third report on educational reform*. Tokyo: Government of Japan.

Pelgrum, W. J., & Plomp, T. (1993). *The IEA study of computers in education: Implementation of an innovation in 21 education systems*. Oxford, UK: Pergamon Press.

Portes, A. (1979). Illegal immigration and the international system, lessons from recent legal Mexican immigrants to the United States. *Social Problems*, 26, 425–443.

Portes, A., McLeod, S., & Parker, R. N. (1978). Immigrant aspirations. *Sociology of Education*, 51, 241–160.

Sakamoto, A., & Sakamoto, T. (1993). Causal relationships between computer use, creativity, and motivation for learning in children: A panel survey of male elementary students. *Educational Technology Research*, 16, 1–10.

Sakamoto, A., Hatano, K., & Sakamoto, T. (1992). Relationships between children's use of computers and psychological variables such as creativity, achievement motivation, and social development. *Japan Journal of Educational Technology*, 15, 143–155.

Sakamoto, T. , Zhao, L., & Sakamoto, A. (1991, May). *Psychological impacts of computers on children*. Paper presented to the fourth International Conference on Children in the Information Age, Albena, Bulgaria.

Urdang, L. (Ed.). (1968). *Dictionary of the English language, college edition*. New York: Random House.

Watanabe, R. & Sawada, T. (1990, April). *The use of computers in Japanese schools*. Paper presented at the annual meeting of the American Educational Research Association, Boston, MA.

Wilder, G., Mackie, D., & Cooper, J. (1985). Gender and computers: Two surveys of computer-related attitudes. *Sex Roles*, 13(3/4), 215–228.

Yawkey, T. D. (1986). The computers in nursery school. *Prospects*, 16(4), 475–480.

Zeleny, R. O. (1990). *Childcraft dictionary*. Chicago: World Book.

Chapter 6

Reflections

Betty A. Collis
Gerald A. Knezek
Kwok-Wing Lai
Keiko T. Miyashita
Willem J. Pelgrum
Tjeerd Plomp
Takashi Sakamoto

This book started with a perspective (written by Collis and Sakamoto) of the context in which the studies in this book occurred. The "Information Age" was sketched, and the role and importance of information technology (IT), and specifically computers in education was focused on. In particular, the benefits of bringing together international studies relating to the impact of computer use in schools on children was noted, in order to examine this impact in the context of different cultures and through the differing lenses of a variety of research methodologies. Chapters 2 through 5 of the book then carried out this task.

But to close the book, we go back to the reflective position that was taken in chapter 1. Stepping back from our own studies and experiences, how do we as individual researchers see the overall domain? What do each of us, individually, see as major trends and insights with respect children and computers in education?

Instead of trying to merge our voices and views into a single closing chapter, we have elected to emphasize our different perspectives, thus making it stronger when the views that emerge from different researchers in different parts of the world seem to converge around major insights. This chapter, therefore presents personal perspectives of the seven authors of this book, not only on the three studies taken together but more generally the impact of computer-related technology on children.

The sections were written independently of each other, yet two main observations seem to emerge. The first is the central importance of the teacher, not the technology, in whatever happens with computer technology in schools. The second is that the role of the teacher, and the educational paradigm underlying that role, must change in order for the potential of IT as a problem-solving tool and as a stimulus for fundamental curriculum change to occur. In their different voices, the researchers, in the six sections that follow in this chapter, seem to each come to these two messages.

The first two of the sections refer more explicitly to a summary of the three studies themselves, whereas the last four of the sections are more focused on the broader perspective of paradigm change in education, one through the lens of changes at the educational system level, one through changes in technology as well as in educational philosophy, one through changes in the role of the teacher, and one through changes at both the teacher and school level. The reflections in different degrees of emphasis and using different words, seem to agree that a paradigm shift from a deterministic to a constructivist and collaborative philosophy of teaching and learning needs to occur. All also agree this shift will take time, but that even now, good things can and are happening with children and computer use in schools.

* * *

REFLECTIONS ON SELECTED RESEARCH TOPICS
(Gerald A. Knezek and Keiko T. Miyashita)

Several contributions to research issues in the field of children and computers in school can be identified from the joint findings of the three studies in this book. Some research questions are left unanswered as well. This section begins with a discussion of the major integrated findings, then proceeds to topics needing further research.

Meta-Findings

1. Computers and related information technologies are being incorporated into daily education practice in virtually every corner of the world.

This finding emerges strongly from the CompEd and YCCI studies, plus much other related research in the field. CompEd data for 1989 versus 1992 shows this general trend among 21 national education systems. The YCCI study has documented how Japan, as one example, made a national policy decision to go from a position of relatively low computer diffusion rates at the elementary school level throughout the 1980s, to one that should put it on par with other technology diffusion leaders, such as the United States, by the mid-1990s (Knezek, Miyashita, & Sakamoto,

1990). It has been demonstrated that other Pacific Basin countries such as Thailand and the Peoples Republic of China are following the same general trend in the diffusion of IT into education as was followed in Japan and the United States, except that diffusion rates in these nations lag behind Japan by roughly the same order of magnitude (about 5 years) that Japan trailed the United States (Knezek et al., 1994; Loipha & Knezek, 1992). Even remote Pacific Island nations are going from a status of little or no IT to large-scale adoption in less than 15 years (Dobrin-Fujiki, Finau, & Knezek, 1995). It seems that most nations will arrive at the same place with regard to adoption of ITs in education, only at slightly different times.

2. Teacher competence and confidence with IT is the principal determinant of effective use.

Researchers conducting the IEA CompEd study found that, among several nations of the world, there has historically been a strong relationship between extent of use of IT in education and formal educator training in its use. ITEC researchers, on the other hand, observed that it is not necessary for exceptional computer-using teachers to have received large amounts of formal computer training. These apparently contradictory findings, when taken in a broader context, both concur with trends observed by YCCI researchers in primary schools: A competent, enthusiastic computer instructor (and often, an enthusiastic principal) was the common theme among diverse applications and environments that teachers, parents, and researchers alike judged to be exceptional. Most YCCI teachers had received some formal training in educational uses of IT. Many had taught themselves. The cause of teacher competence did not seem to be as important as the fact that it existed. A summary statement about the ITEC project seems to apply equally well to YCCI classroom observations related to this area:

> While the style of interaction and teaching and classroom organization varied widely, the image of happy and engaged children, working with and around computers in a productive and confident way, talking to each other, working not independent of the teacher, but on the path that the teacher set for them, comes out again and again. (Collis, personal communication, May 19, 1995)

3. Educationally meaningful exposure to computers in school fosters positive attitudes toward computers.

This finding emerges most strongly from the YCCI study and other quantitative research in the field. However, it is also consistent with ITEC conclusions that the attitudes of the children in the ITEC study were positive while they were using computers in school.

YCCI researchers found a large increase in the extent to which students enjoy using computers and a substantial increase in how important students perceive computers to be for schoolwork and later careers, due to the use of computers in school. The increases attributable to computer exposure for primary school children were at least as great as those found in previous meta-analyses (e.g., C. Kulik & Kulik, 1991) of research studies conducted mainly with older children and adults. These findings strongly reiterate the conclusion reported by J. Kulik (1994) that "students develop more positive attitudes toward computers when they receive help from them in school" (p. 11).

4. Gender differences in knowledge of and attitudes toward computers exist in some nations of the world, especially at the post-primary education level.

The ITEC study found no particular indications of gender differences in the effect of IT on higher cognitive processes, but the CompEd study found large instances of male dominance in some nations with respect to attitudes toward and knowledge of IT. YCCI found no consistent gender differences in Grades 1 through 3 with respect to attitudes toward computers or any of the other four psychological dispositions measured, except for empathy,[1] which stands out as the sole instance among the three studies in this book where females were consistently higher than males. However, in the case of empathy, there was no indication that gender differences are strongly related to use of IT.

We can summarize these and many other researchers' findings by stating there is little doubt that gender differences in attitudes toward computers and knowledge of IT exist (or, at least did exist in 1992) at postprimary age levels in many nations of the world. These often emerge by lower secondary school (junior high), and generally remain pronounced at the upper secondary (high school) level. Results from two of the three studies forming the basis of this book are generally consistent with a growing body of findings from other sources regarding gender and computers. In a review of the existing literature on this topic, Nelson and Watson (1991, cited in Nelson & Watson, 1994) concluded the following:

> A discernible sex-typed pattern of development in computer use and attitudes has been identified in a number of research studies. In preschool and the early elementary grades, no significant sex-typed differences are apparent. By the third or fourth grade, however, disparities in attitudes and performance scores between girls and boys show that girls seem less technologically motivated and, thus, less interested in future computing experiences. This trend becomes even more pronounced in high school. By adolescence, girls are reported to develop an ardent dislike for computers while boys' enjoyment and skill levels increase. (p. 185)

Having said this, we must also observe that the general statements just given are just generalizations and do not necessarily place the issue of gender and computers in its proper context. Exceptions to the trends may be especially significant in understanding gender differences within cultural contexts. For example, in the CompEd study, Japan at the upper secondary level was the only instance of female students clearly being more positive about the relevance of computers than males

---

[1]Defined by YCCI researchers as a caring concern for the thoughts and feelings of others.

(Janssen Reinen & Plomp, 1993b, p. 97). Six other systems at the upper secondary level, seven national education systems at the lower secondary level, and two systems at the elementary level, all had average attitudes of males higher than females. Follow-up inquiries with the CompEd researchers for Japan (Sakamoto, personal communication, June 6, 1995) revealed that upper secondary Japanese females involved in the CompEd study were frequently from business (vocational) high schools where they routinely use IT for career-related training. This may explain why the attitudes of this female group tended to be highly positive, compared to their male counterparts, who were more equally dispersed among vocational and academic high schools. Perceived usefulness may be a much stronger factor in determining attitudes toward computers than any general male or female gender bias.

Other less striking but equally relevant contrasts from the CompEd study exist in the area of computer enjoyment. The average rating on attitudes toward computers for males was higher than females in all countries surveyed, but for Japan and the United States in elementary education, and India in upper secondary education, the male–female differences were not significant (Janssen Reinen & Plomp, 1993b, p. 97). Because IEA findings were derived from large numbers of student responses (the average sample size for a given level in a national education system was 3,363 students), failure to reach statistical significance can be interpreted as strong evidence for no meaningful difference. One must wonder if there is some special characteristic of the environments of these nations that promotes male–female equity, at least on this one, very narrow, issue.

It is also noteworthy that the IEA CompEd study found the difference between genders in knowledge of computers was not so great in the absolute sense. The largest average gender difference on the Functional Information Technology Test was less than 3 questions out of 27, for any education level in any nation (Janssen Reinen & Plomp, 1993b, p. 94). So perhaps the CompEd findings are not so much at odds with ITEC researchers who observed no obvious gender differences with respect to meaningful use of IT, after all. Gender differences that exist with regard to knowledge of and meaningful use of IT in education may be quite small.

Interesting But Unanswered Questions

Interaction of Home and School Use.   CompEd is the only one of the three studies in this book that gathered hard data on this topic. The indications from CompEd analyses are that there is an interaction between home and school computer use, but type, direction, and spheres of influence are not yet well-defined. Some previous research in the field has favored the common-sense notion that combined computer use at school and at home can be beneficial to learning-related psychological dispositions (e.g., Sakamoto & Sakamoto, 1993), but other research has concluded that students who are computer game users at home can sometimes become disillusioned about computer use in school (e.g., King, 1994–1995). More research needs to be carried out before definitive statements can be made in this area.

Is the Novelty Effect Real?   Previous research has provided convincing arguments that students develop less positive attitudes toward computers as they use them longer in school (Krendl & Broihier, 1992; Wilder, Mackie, & Cooper, 1985). The CompEd study described in this book also provides some evidence for this trend. However, YCCI analyses indicate that the commonly reported "novelty effect for computers," which is a tendency for students to tire of the computer as if it were a new toy, may actually be a secondary effect of less positive attitudes toward schooling in general, with increasing age/grade advances, which in turn can lead to lower absolute perceptions of certain kinds of attitudes toward computers. That is, computers in school may be just one of the many facets of schooling in general that come to be less positively perceived as students advance to higher grade levels. More research is needed to determine the underlying causes of declines in attitudes toward computers, when they are found to exist.

Long-Term Effect on Student Cognition and Achievement.   The YCCI study found evidence that meaningful computer exposure, over several years, can have a positive impact on students' motivation for learning (study habits and motivation/persistence), and we make the assumption that this will eventually have a positive impact on indices such as standardized measures of school achievement. In the ITEC study, there were positive comments by both principals and teachers (e.g., Collis, 1993) about the positive effects of computer activities on students' cognitive processes such as metacognition, problem solving, and creativity. Nevertheless, it is not clear in which direction, or from what source, causality springs in these areas. For example, there is some evidence from YCCI analyses that creative children come to perceive computer use as important, rather than a perception of enhanced computer importance (which follows from increased use) leading to more creative tendencies. Much more research needs to be carried out to resolve these complex questions of causation. As concluded by the ITEC researchers, one of the most complex issues appears to be simply how to define and measure the concept of *higher level cognitive functions.*

Impact on Local Culture.   Ample evidence exists in the popular press that television from first world nations influences third world national cultures. Scholars such as Bower (1988) pointed out there is no reason to believe the prepackaged "easy" applications described by CompEd researchers in this book, such as drill and practice CAI, will be any different. This type of software is typically translated directly from a native language such as English, into a foreign language, without regard for the differences in culture. Rewards and examples are sometimes inappropriate according to local standards, and may inadvertently teach children who use such software an alien value system.

On the other hand, it also appears that "noneasy" tool, simulation, microworld, or computer-mediated communications environments, which require local, teacher-aided implementation in every nation, quickly take on a local flavor that is not only unique but also frequently adopted as a model by educators in other parts of the world. Several examples of this type emerged from among the teachers and researchers involved in the ITEC project (see, e.g., Lazarova, 1993; Rubstov, 1990; Tzoneva & Collis, 1992), and the largest nations/states do not necessarily hold a monopoly on innovative applications. For example, computer-mediated communi-cation curricula from island nations or states such as New Zealand and Hawaii, have been adopted in far-away nations such as Great Britain, Israel, Russia, and Slovakia (Christensen, Clayton, Campbell, & Knezek, 1994; Knezek, Southworth, Christensen, Jones, & Moore, 1995; Young, Gullickson-Morfitt, & Southworth, 1993). It is possible that IT may eventually "empower" smaller or less developed nations to not only better determine their local educational environments, but also to lead global educational initiatives, if they so choose.

Murray-Lasso (1993) from Mexico has provided an eloquent description of the ways in which local culture can influence and be influenced by the introduction of IT into education. His essay was written for the ITEC Project but applies equally well to all three studies reported in this book. In the current context, it is sufficient to state that we strongly concur with his conclusion that "it is urgent to do more research on the cultural aspects of the use of computers in education" (Murray-Lasso, 1993, p. 5.3-26). The complete text of Murray-Lasso's paper, entitled "Culture as a Context and Determinant of Educational uses of Information Tech-nology," is reproduced in the appendix for the interested reader.

Possible Negative Side Effects Across Cultures. Our summary of find-ings should not conclude without addressing the issue of possible universal negative effects of using IT in schools. From ITEC there seems to be no evidence of negative side effects on students. CompEd also found none. However, neither of these studies was specifically searching for any. YCCI looked for a negative impact on children's empathy and found none, but exploratory data analysis that included middle school (lower secondary) subjects appears to have found a tendency for some students to use the computer as a place to hide from their daily problems, such as schoolwork or difficult social interactions (Knezek & Miyashita, 1994). In addition, anecdotal evidence gathered by YCCI researchers concurs with findings in Australia by King (1994–1995) that some 11- to 12-year-old children appear to suffer from "with-drawal symptoms" from computer games and acquire negative attitudes toward computers when confined to educationally relevant uses of computers in schools. In the words of King (1994–1995):

> [high computer anxiety] students appeared to separate themselves into two camps—those who were concerned with the lack of access and wanted more access so they could learn more, and those whose initial and continuing expectations of computers were focused on games. The concern of this second group was related to the way they were being weaned from games, resulting in some disillusionment and a reversal of opinion about computers. (pp. 165–166)

Based on this and other research in the field, it seems premature to conclude that the use of IT in education is devoid of undesirable side effects. Our best conjecture is that isolated overuse to the point of infringing on a young child's normal explorations with physical manipulatives (building blocks, etc.), reducing cooperative play with human peers, or restricting opportunities for physical exercise, is unhealthy and unwise. However, we know of no concrete evidence that the small number of hours per week a typical student currently works with computers in school places him or her in our hypothesized "danger" category.

The most important issue in the area of negative side effects seems to be a concern for possible long-range negative impacts of IT on the current generation of children, after they take their places as productive citizens in their respective societies. Unfortunately, conclusive answers to these kinds of questions may require studies much more longitudinal in nature than those represented in this book. Presently, the long-range effect of introducing IT in education is unknown. It is conceivable that, in 15 years, follow-up studies on some of the CompEd, ITEC, or YCCI children may help answer this question.

* * *

MEASURING THE EFFECTS OF COMPUTERS
IN EDUCATION: METHODS AND RESULTS
(Betty A. Collis)

In this section, I offer some personal reflections at a global level as a personal view of how the three studies reported in this book harmonize and support each other. This personal view is focused on two main points of reflection: reflection on the methodologies of the studies, and what these studies offer in terms of strategies for future research projects, and on key findings from the three studies, focusing particularly on culture.

How Can We Measure the Impact of Computer
Use in Education on a Cross-Cultural Basis?

CompEd, ITEC, and YCCI shared many concerns and many interests. As researchers, the members of the three projects shared a common concern for finding an effective methodology to validly and objectively capture cross-cultural differences relating to various aspects of children and computer use. Appropriate to their research questions and their backgrounds, the studies used different approaches and instrumentation. CompEd and YCCI were similar in that they relied on fixed-response instruments administered to large samples. ITEC differed, in that it used a large range of observational data as well as a battery of instruments, and a case study approach where, by definition, the interpretation of the local researcher was interwoven in the data and its interpretation. But in all three studies, the methodology was agreed upon by researchers with long and proven experience in dealing with methodological issues, instrument development, sampling, and data analysis.

Two general questions present themselves when looking at the methodology of the three studies: Can we, based on our experience from the three studies, make a recommendation for methodology for subsequent studies? Were culture and cross-cultural differences handled adequately in the studies?

Choice of Methodology. It is well known that the choice of methodology for a research study must reflect the research questions of the study. The three studies in this book, although dealing with the same overall domain, had very different research questions and each chose a methodology that fit its focus. It does not seem debatable to say that if one wants an overview of broadscale patterns of usage, one should choose a survey technique and if one wants to study the dynamics of a classroom then one should choose a mixture of observational techniques.

Yet it is also well known that whatever technique is chosen, something is lost. The broader the view, the less feeling of life; the closer the immersion in life, the less the ability to generalize and summarize. Clearly, what this book shows is that a variety of methods, taken in combination, is what is best: overview data, systematically gathered, complimented by qualitative and observational data, also systematically gathered. Together these two can bring frame and interpretation closer into synchrony. A consideration of the videotapes of classroom and school culture collected by ITEC shows clearly the difficulties in capturing the richness of computer-use situations, certainly in broadscale inventory-type surveys but also in naturalistic case studies. The three studies in this book suggest the strength of a single study combining both approaches.

Such a single study is probably not likely to occur. The costs and difficulties of mounting such a study make it unlikely; the extent to which IT is now integrated into schools and society further confounds the difficulties of motivating a study to measure its effects. Of the three studies in this book, the only one with a stable funding basis was CompEd. ITEC depended heavily on the impact of UNESCO in many of its participating countries. Ironically, with the change in governments in the East European countries that occurred during the ITEC period, the UNESCO organizations in those countries lost much of their established framework for stimulating research activities making it now very difficult to find a nongovernmental organization with influence to support a research project on a worldwide level.

The cost-effectiveness of a methodology must also be considered. The ITEC study involved nine international meetings, at a considerable cost, both in time and finances. Even so, this was not enough to fully extract and interpret indicators and messages in the data. The survey-type approaches such as in CompEd and YCCI are more manageable and efficient, but each also involved considerable organization and expense, particularly so with CompEd, where the responsibility of summarizing countries requires considerable national support and conviction that the national research team can in fact represent the country in its sampling. As with any research, the costs of the activity must be considered against its payoff. Payoff is related to validity and generalizability, but also insight and relevance to decision making.

Taken together, the three studies in this book do bring many insights that can be extremely helpful to decision makers. In terms of recommendations for the methodology for any future multinational study about IT and education, it seems important to blend the range of perspectives in these three studies: system, classroom, and individual learner, and the range of methodologies: survey and systematic observation. The question of feasibility remains. What agency will support the cost and complexity of such an integrated approach?

A further comment about validity and reliability is suggested by the three studies. Each was carried out, as carefully as was possible, in a way sensitive to the need to support the validity and reliability of its methods. It would seem that the CompEd and YCCI studies have more reliable methods than the ITEC study, if reliability is given its textbook definition of reproducibility and objectivity.

Yet, such a conclusion should not be taken too quickly. Every step in a research study is saturated by its researchers, if they are physically present in the data-collection process as they were in ITEC, or far distant, as they were in CompEd and YCCI. As an example, the relationship of gender and computer use stands out. CompEd and YCCI researchers asked questions about gender, analyzed their data according to gender, and found conclusions about gender. ITEC researchers did not ask particular questions about gender, did not see gender emerge as a differentiating aspect of computer use in its classrooms, and thus did not come to any conclusion about gender. Which approach is more objective? Neither is to be criticized. The example is only to show that researchers always determine the lens and filter through which conclusions are drawn.

Again, the recommendation seems to be to combine a number of lenses, as is occurring in this book, and then see what comes through this variety of lenses most consistently.

Culture.   A major common aspect of each of the three studies in this book is their cross-cultural basis. Each wishes in its own ways to examine the impact of culture on the phenomenon of computer use in schools and its impact on learners. ITEC in particular began with considerable discussion of what is meant by culture, and which aspects of culture should be taken as a frame for the subsequent research. Family? Socioeconomic class? Ethnic group? Race? Religion? Political aspects? All of these are well-known determiners of culture.

Despite the frustrations of some of its originals researchers, ITEC came to the conclusion that it was not possible to carry out analysis based on these aspects of culture. Some of the reasons were methodological and procedural; others related to the eventual complexity of handling the interpretation of the data. Thus, ITEC chose to define "culture" by "country." This has been generally the approach in the other two studies, although CompEd prefers to speak of educational systems instead of countries as units of analysis, thus reflecting at least some of the major cultural differences in countries such as Canada and Belgium. YCCI has done the most insightful work with the culture variable, by studying bilingual Hispanic students living in the United States. Thus most of the conclusions that can be made about culture in the three studies in this book assume that culture is equivalent to national affiliation. This simplification was practical and justifiable for all three studies, given their research questions and their backgrounds. The YCCI work with Hispanic students in the United States, and the ITEC observations of common elements in classroom cultures when computers are in use, across national boundaries, suggest that further cross-cultural studies need both national definitions of culture but also something more meaningful to the actual experience of the learner.

The Studies in Combination: What Messages Come Through From All of Them?

The three studies in this book, with their three different perspectives and their different methodologies, give us an important opportunity for triangulation of their results. This cannot be taken too far, however, because of the differences in their research questions and thus in the questions they asked in their procedures. It seems clear from the studies that:

- Computer use in schools is increasingly established in schools around the world (a result well supported by many other indicators).
- At the system level, predictable issues and problems arise.
- At the classroom level, teachers are choosing from a variety of ways to make use of IT, including not to make use of it at all.
- From the learner level (at least for younger children), children are motivated by using the technology, are not negatively affected by it, and seem to be benefiting from it.

Although these conclusions seem simple, they are in fact profound, given the intense speculation about the impact of computers in education that occurred in the late 1970s and early 1980s.

These conclusions seem to be relatively clear after reviewing the three studies. As an individual I also have personal conclusions about the impact of computer use on children that I see emerging from the three studies in this book, and from my more general experience. I close my portion of this reflection chapter with my own list of key results:

1. Regardless of systemwide approach, major results seem the same.

During the 1980s, at the system level, intense efforts went on in many countries to find optimal ways at the system level of introducing and supporting IT in schools. What the three studies in this book, taken together, show is that despite all the variations in strategy at the system level that have occurred, similar problems and issues are still present, a wide range of classroom and teacher responses to IT is still occurring, and there is no consistent evidence that children, looked at from a system (i.e., country) level, are responding differently because of national policies. This, if it is a justified conclusion from the three studies taken in combination, is a result that is quite amazing. Perhaps it is too bold to claim. But at least in the ITEC study, the impact of national policy and strategy did not seem to have any reflection in the classrooms that were observed. Regardless of great differences in national strategy and policy among the 17 studies whose classrooms were observed for the full term of ITEC, the ITEC researchers saw great commonalities in what was going on, in terms of happy and engaged children and dedicated and innovative teachers.

2. Regardless of many variables at the classroom level and software level, the teacher is the critical influence.

And what about the classroom level? An enormous amount of research has gone on with respect to teacher training, to approaches for the instructional integration of computers in the classroom, to software characteristics, and to issues relating to innovation in the classroom. Something quite important does seem to emerge from the combination of the three studies in this book in this respect. In the CompEd study, with its broad sampling, the definite tendency toward the use of "easy" applications of computers was supported; easy in the sense of easy to integrate into existing classroom practice, easy to fit to existing curricula and methods, easy for learners to use in a self-supporting way. Game playing and drill and practice are the major uses of the computers that have made their way into elementary schools. Because these activities are by definition time-intensive and computer-intensive relative to their use (e.g., a child must sit, by him or herself, for a certain period of time at a computer if drill is to be effective), the most predictable, and reasonable, response from a system level is "We need more computers."

But the ITEC study shows a very different situation. When one examines not the "average" classroom, but the "special" situation where a combination of circumstances, largely influenced by the characteristics of the individual teacher, has led to substantial use of computers in the learning practice, what we saw was very different than the CompEd picture. In ITEC we saw almost no game playing. We saw almost no drill and practice. We heard almost no complaints that more hardware was needed. Instead we saw teachers making the successful effort to integrate computer use in the whole lesson experience, not as a supplementary drill or diversion, but as a learning media with which the whole class was engaged. This does not have to occur through sitting each child in front of a computer at the same time, although it can, but can also occur through use of a single computer as an important resource during a lesson, which learners use as a reference tool or a production tool or a data-accumulating tool. Such approaches do not necessarily require more computers; they do necessarily require a teacher willing to change his or her instructional method to incorporate the strengths of the technology.

That this does not yet often occur at the system level is borne out by the CompEd study. That this can occur in the classroom level, with rich consequences, is borne out by the ITEC study. The studies do not contradict each other; each is necessary to see the whole picture.

3. Regardless of different experiences and cultures, children are benefiting from and enjoying their use of computers.

With regard to the individual, all the studies concur. Children are learning with and about computers, regardless of what happens at the system and even classroom level. Children find computers interesting and not threatening, despite our earlier fears. Children can handle computers in a way parallel to the evolution of computer use in their larger societies. Children are not being negatively affected by technology in their schools, at least in any way we can capture in these data. These are very good things to report; thousands of words of concern have been expressed about these issues over the last 15 years; considerable effort has gone into the development of a range of different programs and curricula for introducing children to computers in schools. Perhaps we can say, it doesn't seem to matter; perhaps we can say it has all contributed to a positive evolution. What does matter is that for the child, the use of computers in schools is generally a positive experience, both subjectively and in some unmeasurable way, intellectually. This is very good news.

4. Regardless of methodological approach, there is no simple answer about how to best use computers in education.

More specifically, the studies taken in combination bring both good news and frustrating news to decision makers. Frustrating news, in that no "simple" answers emerge with regard to actual steps and decisions. No one type of educational software can be clearly shown to be "most effective." No one approach to teacher training can be shown to be most useful. No clear indication about how many computers of what type should be present in a school can be claimed. No clear evidence of learning effect, relative to classic indicators such as systemwide improvement in normalized test scores or job market indicators, can yet be substantiated on a broadscale basis among countries with respect to computer use in schools. No particular evidence favors one strategy for national policy to another. No particular classroom procedure is to be consistently recommended as "the best way" to make use of computers.

5. Despite what we don't know, we can believe that good things are happening.

But the frustration of these results is also their strength. Technology is moving into schools, (some) teachers are making use of the technology, children are benefiting. We can and we must continue, with a positive and confident feeling.

* * *

THE EDUCATIONAL POTENTIAL OF NEW
INFORMATION TECHNOLOGIES:
WHERE ARE WE NOW?
(Willem J. Pelgrum)

For many countries only 10 years have passed since microcomputers started to be introduced into schools, and numerous research projects have been conducted to monitor these developments and to determine the educational effects of them. My reflections can be summarized as follows.

In the beginning of the 1980s when the introduction of personal computers started, there was speculation about the educational potential of new ITs for changing education into a much more stimulating and motivating study environ‐ ment than it had been before. Although, since then, rapid changes took place in terms of the availability of hardware and software in schools, most of what has happened for education at large in countries seems to be a cosmetic change. Really substantial changes have not yet been observed.

When looking back in time, it is interesting to mention the skepticism of some reviewers, when the IEA CompEd study was launched in 1984: The data would be obsolete at the moment of publication. Although the study results showed that part of this criticism was correct (the availability of hardware in schools was indeed rapidly changing), from the point of view of educational change, this skepticism proved to be hardly tenable. For the vast majority of students in most countries, computer use takes place in the margins of the educational process.

This observation confirms that educational changes proceed very slowly. Experts in the field of educational innovations are not surprised by this finding. It is what they expected on the basis of experiences with many other large‐scale innovations. Education reacts as a mammoth tanker; it has a high mass and cannot perform sudden maneuvers. Although the pace of developments with regard to new ITs may be disappointing from the point of view of the rather naive optimistic fortune tellers from the early 1980s, the findings reported in this book are worthwhile for several reasons. First, they taught us something about the practice of educational use of new ITs and deepened our insight in this process of educational innovation, while at the same time allowing us to create databases that are of high historical value because they contain a systematically collected set of data describing the infant phase of new ITs in education. Second, the findings may help us in mitigating overly high expectations of the educational potential of recently introduced technologies (such as telematics and multimedia).

Although the slow pace of the infusion of new ITs in education illustrates the inertia of the educational system at large, on the other hand it also shows that there is still progress. The question is how long this progress will continue. Future research will uncover the answer. I am quite convinced that any substantial educational change requires at least:

1. A specification of clear and relevant goals that are seen as important by educational politicians and educational practitioners.

2. A system of continuous teacher training.
3. The availability of practical lesson materials that have a clear link with the goals.
4. A continuous system of monitoring the implementation and progress of the change, with adequate feedback mechanisms for the practitioners involved in the innovation process.
5. A transparent demonstration of the added value of the innovation in terms of educational outcomes that are valued by educational practitioners and society at large.

One conclusion from the large-scale studies that have been conducted so far is that none of the conditions stated here have been implemented sufficiently in the countries under study. A side observation from what has been said previously is that apparently there is a high need for educational change toward a more interesting and stimulating learning environment that prepares youngsters adequately for their future lives. It seems that the challenge for all who are involved in further stimulating new ITs in education should be focused on this goal. So, we should not use new ITs as a technology about which students need to learn, but as a tool for promoting educational change.

* * *

FUTURE RESEARCH NEEDS AND OPPORTUNITIES
(Takashi Sakamoto)

New Technologies for Networking and Multimedia

CompEd, ITEC, and YCCI were conducted in the early 1990s. Before that, computers as research objects were rather primitive and simple and had no suitable functions for multimedia technologies. In the mid-1990s, multimedia and network technologies are being widely introduced into educational fields. Advanced schools have some excellent machines with CD-ROMs that can be utilized for multimedia. Sometimes they are connected to each other with LANs and the Internet. Some schools already access the Internet and multimedia with excellent software such as Mosaic and CU–SeeMe through the World Wide Web (WWW). These kinds of technology uses are usually supported by governments. Examples such as the National Information Infrastructure (NII) and National Research and Education Network (NREN) in the United States and the "100 Schools Project" in Japan are well known. Several schools in the world have joined the Global Schoolhouse Project.

Multimedia systems are a combination between information-processing technology by computers and audiovisual IT such as CD-ROM, MIDI, and other devices. Computer-supported collaborative work environments (CSCW) and distance learning are also utilized. In the near future, these multimedia and network technologies will become popular in school education. Teachers and students will be able to easily exchange information such as data, pictures, tables, sentences, and music across cultural and national boundaries.

The following are anticipated activities in schools utilizing multimedia and network technologies.

1. Tools for Communication
   * Multimedia data gathering by retrieving from remote information resources
   * Audiovisual presentation including sound, voice, text, tables, graphs, pictures, photos, moving images, etc.
   * Multimedia information exchanges with schools in other parts of the world.
   * CSCW including cooperative problem solving, composing music and sentences, drawings, etc.
2. Tools for Intellectual Activities
   * Discovery of principles and rules in natural and social phenomena through multimedia simulation and games
   * Problem solving at a distance
   * Cooperative creation such as composing and editing sentences, music design, pictures, drawings at a distance
   * Measuring natural and social phenomena such as weather, pollution, traffic, etc. around the world
   * Controlling robots and machines at a distance

By using multimedia and network technologies, children may acquire abilities and competencies for thinking, problem solving, information presentation, composition, cognitive skills, knowledge, computer ethics such as privacy and piracy, and cooperative work among children in the world. Especially the impact on the child might be greater in the multimedia technology period than it was in the computer technology period.

Based on the research currently reported we can plan to undertake new research on the psychological and instructional impacts of multimedia and network technologies on children. These include how multimedia and network technologies effect computer enjoyment, motivation for learning, attitudes toward computer use, computer relevance, higher level cognitive abilities, and skills possessed by the children of the world.

We can also anticipate that cooperative research itself will be done through the Internet. For example, questionnaire surveys and interviews can be conducted. Just as multimedia and network technologies open education to the world and make all schools in different countries into one worldwide school, so do the same technologies also make it possible for individual research projects to become one worldwide cooperative activity. It may soon be possible for CompEd, ITEC and YCCI teams to join together to cooperate in one integrated new research team on the Impact of Multimedia on Children.

Influence of Educational Philosophy

Human learning has changed from traditional indoctrination to behaviorism and also to cognitive constructivism. From the traditional viewpoint, children passively learned things from information given by teachers. Therefore, chalk and black-board, and audiovisual educational technologies were often utilized. But from the behavioristic viewpoint, children can learn gradually but actively by accumulating bits of programmed information successively given by teachers. Therefore, CAI such as drill and practice and tutorial mode have often been made and utilized.

Recently, the situation has been changing based on cognitive constructivism. From this viewpoint, children acquire their own knowledge and concepts based on the integration of their own previous experiences and information given from the external environment. Therefore, computer uses are also changing. Children initiate use of and actively employ computers as tools for problem solving, data retrieval, discovering principles and rules of natural and social phenomena, measuring natural phenomena, and controlling robots and machines. Future research on children and computers must take into account such shifts in educational paradigms.

* * *

LIVING IN THE INFORMATION AGE
(Kwok-Wing Lai)

Although it is difficult to measure the exact impact of the rapidly expanding use of information and communication technologies in society there is no doubt that these technologies have already had a significant effect on education. One question of great concern to us is: What is the role of the school in the information society and how does it respond to all these technological changes? Can the educational system, the schools, the curriculum, the principals and teachers respond quickly enough to the change of job requirements, study requirements, literacy expectations so as to provide a rich and creative learning environment to prepare the learners for these changes? The first question that comes to our mind, after we have reviewed findings from the studies, is therefore what is actual happening in schools in this rapidly changing technological society?

There is little doubt that in the last decade or so the educational system has tried to respond to these changing requirements in several different ways. For example, as reported in the IEA CompEd study, there have been an increase of availability of computer hardware and software in schools and there has been a variety of applications in the instructional process at different levels. Teachers also respond in their own ways. We have seen from the ITEC studies that even though some of the participating classes were far from what could be described as technology-rich, some teachers have put the computer to good use. We have seen something good has resulted in several curriculum innovation and exemplary cases. On the curriculum level, new school subjects such as computer studies and computer programming have been added to the curriculum, and almost in every country some kind of pre- and inservice teaching training on computer applications have been institutionalized. In some countries (e.g., in the United States), computer literacy has become a requirement in the teacher certification process.

With all these innovative practices, however, sadly, by and large, computers have not been fully integrated in the daily practice of the average classroom. From the findings reported in our studies there has been little evidence to suggest that computers were widely used in the learning process. It is apparent that most school administrators and teachers do not realize the exciting possibilities these new technologies could offer in restructuring the learning process and there is a lack of vision of what could or could not be done by the use of these new technologies. Even the recent explosion of network communication and the use of the Internet may only represent yet another misguided belief that simply getting on to the net itself may do something good to the students. From what we have observed and reported in the literature we are afraid that even computer networking may go through what Cuban (1986) described as the expectations, rhetoric, policies, and limited-use cycle and after the initial excitement has gone the ripples will disappear.

A variety of reasons could be suggested to account for the limited use of computers in the majority of classrooms. Lack of computer hardware and software is an obvious reason. Some studies (e.g., Watson, 1993) suggest that there may be some minimum threshold of IT use before any noticeable effects can be detected, which implies that more hardware and software is needed in schools. However, findings from our studies, particularly from the ITEC study, show that innovative computer applications do not require a large number of computer hardware or software. The ITEC experience tells us that we should shift our focus from the availability of computing resources (many people still think that this is the most important issue in computers in education) to training and support of teachers who are willing to use the technology in their classrooms. If our focus is on hardware and software we could be easily misled into believing that the technology itself is the solution. Many ITEC classrooms were not technology-rich classrooms (they may only have one or two computers per class). It was only because the technology was carefully integrated into the existing curriculum that something good was identified by most ITEC researchers. So without asking why we computerize our classrooms we do not believe that rapid computerization of classroom is the solution.

The need for teacher support and training stood out as an important factor for the successful integration of IT in the curriculum, as documented both in ours and in some other studies (see, e.g., Sheingold & Hadley, 1990; Watson, 1993). But we have to be careful to distinguish between different kinds of professional development as simply more training does not necessarily mean better teaching. We have observed that although some teachers have received training on how to use IT and may even be encouraged to integrate the technology into the existing curriculum what they actually do is to treat IT as an add-on, yet another tool in their teaching repertoire, and try to fit it into their current practices, or use it to support the teaching style to which they are accustomed.

We believe professional development or training should not stop at the technical level of knowledge and skill acquisition or at the curriculum level where issues of implementation become the only focus of training. Rather, professional development in IT should encourage a shift of values: from a teacher-centered to a student-centered learning process. It is our view that the attitudes and educational philosophies of the teachers that form part of the school culture is a significant factor of whether computers will be used, and how they will be used in schools.

In our view, although IT can be used in a wide variety of situations its potential in education mainly lies in its ability to support and encourage a more learner-centered environment. We believe that the use of information and communication technologies in schools can be emancipative for both teachers and learners. For teachers, IT opens up a new teaching style where they no longer need to impart knowledge to their students. Instead, IT provides opportunities for students to acquire knowledge and skills, access online databases, solve real-world problems, communicate with experts and engage themselves in "teleapprenticeship" schemes. Communication networks such as the Internet also open up a window to the world for students so that global cooperation becomes a possibility. The classroom therefore is extended outside its four walls and becomes a learning community where the learner is at the same time the researcher (Brown, 1994). Learning becomes truly situated where there is a meaningful context for learning to occur.

This represents a shift of values for teachers because learning is no longer seen as confined to four stone walls and the teacher is no longer the sole owner of knowledge. The power relationship in the class has to be changed as the teachers may have to learn side by side with their students. Information technology is seen not as an add-on to the curriculum but as a tool to help restructure the learning process and help build the learning community. Learning therefore is also seen as mainly a collaborative process. Teachers need to realize that their role in a computer-supported learning environment is not so much to impart knowledge and skills to students as to provide guidance and support to them. They have to be the coordinator, the helper, the facilitator, as well as the coach of the learning environment (Lai, 1993). Teachers are there to build a learning community for their students where they are guided in the discovery process and pushed beyond their "natural level" of competence, with the aid of computer networks as well as other powerful tools (Brown, 1994). Computing practices reflect the teaching styles of the teachers. IT offers opportunities to create a totally new relationship between teachers and learners. It is perhaps because teachers are not willing to give up their control, or may be because they feel too threatened to be challenged by this new relationship, which helps to explain why IT is not being used more creatively and innovatively in most classrooms.

* * *

FUTURE DIRECTIONS FOR IT EDUCATION
(Tjeerd Plomp)

Advice and recommendations about IT in education can be given to several categories of people, for example (a) to educational policymakers at the macrolevel of our systems (those who decide on budgets at the system level etc.); (b) to curriculum and courseware developers (who decide on priorities in these areas); (c) to (inservice) teacher trainers (who decide on what is being taught to teachers); (d) to district, local, and/or school administrators (who are setting priorities in meso- and microlevels); and perhaps to others as well. The recommendations that follow are not targeted toward any particular constituency or group, although they might have been. The same recommendations may apply differently to the various constituencies concerned with education.

Recommendations Concerning the Future of Technology in Education

1. More attention needs to be paid to applications that really do enhance learning.

Computers/new IT can be used in education for many purposes, such as drill and practice, learning new materials (tutorials), or as a tool, for example: word processing, spreadsheet, and database. All these applications are very powerful for more traditional educational settings and objectives: the learning of facts and theories. But to use the computer to enhance learning, as a tool that is to support problem-solving skills (or higher order or productive skills; or a more constructivist approach to teaching and learning), applications like simulations, modeling, computer-based laboratory, and so forth, are needed, through which students are challenged to solve problems and construct their knowledge, while the computer supports the activity by doing time-consuming and/or labor-intensive parts. The CompEd data show that most computer use is tutorial, drill and practice and the use of word processing, while simulations, modeling and microcomputer-based laboratories hardly occur.

2. Stimulation policies need to be aimed at full integration of the computers/new IT in all educational processes and not just at having computers having "passed the front door of the schools."

CompEd data show that computers have gained their place in the schools. Schools can hardly be envisaged without computers. But this study also shows that the use of computers is still limited in several ways. First, most use in schools is by teaching a course in (introductory) computer education. Second, a majority of teachers in "existing" subject matter areas are not yet using computers. And third, the type of use is such that it cannot be expected to strongly support the development of problem-solving/higher order skills. If policymakers really want computers/new IT to be integrated into education, they need to stimulate its use in all classrooms and should not be satisfied that computer use stops at most classroom doors.

3. An equity perspective is important for organizing computer use in schools. The CompEd study shows that girls are less stimulated by their parents to work with computers; they have also less access to computers outside school. Therefore:
4. Strategies for introduction of computers in education/schools need to be based on a long-term vision/perspective. As previously reported, most use in computer education involves limited integration and is low-level use. This is all okay, if one has a long-term perspective of how computers should be infused in teaching and learning. Then easy uses are acceptable. Without such a long-term perspective, the full potential of computers/new IT will never be realized.
5. Stimulation of courseware development, as well as teacher (inservice) training need to take into account the present limitations of the hardware and software infrastructure in the schools. Imagine what kind of infrastructure would be needed if every teacher would want to use computers in every (or let us say half of his or her lessons). The present limitations (e.g., for as long as computers are not as generally available as calculators) make that not even thinkable.
6. As real integration of computers/new IT in education is a very complex innovation, it may not only require intensive and long inservice training, but it may also involve re-designing major parts of our present education system. Real integration means major changes: (a) from teacher centered teaching to student-centered teaching ⇒ other beliefs, and other didactical repertoire needed; (b) paying much more attention to problem-solving/higher order skills ⇒ new teaching materials complex in comparison to the "traditional" ones; (c) other organizational structures for the school: more project work, cooperative learning ⇒ other organization patterns, even other physical arrangements, other time organization, and so on. Real change is asking for change that is multidimensional and policymakers, administrators, teacher (inservice) trainers, and so forth need to take this into account when they making policies and planning implementation.

Why Information Technology in Schools?

One major question stated in the opening chapter is why IT would or should get a place in schools. Policymakers (on whatever level in the system) may have their reasons why they want schools dealing with IT, but it is in the schools that the policymakers' "why" will be operationalized. Will it be a minimal operationalization, where schools try to meet the policymakers' expectations with minimal efforts and minimal disruption of the existing daily routine? Or do we find optimal usage of the potentials of IT in education. It is therefore important to discuss the "why" question in the context of the "how" question. At first, we reflect on the "why" question. Then the results presented in the previous chapters are discussed in the context of the "why" question.

The studies presented in this book took place in a period during which the use of IT in schools, which was at that time mainly the use of computers, reflected several policy perspectives. Using Hawkridge's (1991) labels (see chapter 1), these are the social, the vocational, and the pedagogical rationale. The social rationale is important, as it reflects the belief that students should be prepared to deal with computers, or more generally with IT, in order to become well-informed citizens. The vocational rationale implies that students need to be prepared to use computers for future jobs, and the pedagogical rationale that computers can improve and enhance the teaching and learning processes. School principals mention as the most important reasons for introducing computers in their schools "to give students experience with computers that they will need in the future" and "to keep the curriculum and methods up-to-date" (Pelgrum, Janssen Reinen, & Plomp, 1993, p. 29). These reasons refer to both the social and pedagogical rationale. That the vocational rationale is not being reflected in the studies reported in this book is not surprising, as all three studies are mainly focused at general education (only in the CompEd study some vocational schools were included in the survey, but also this study was primarily oriented on the use of computers in general subjects such as mathematics, science, and mother tongue). But it is known from other sources that in all industrialized countries the vocational rationale has been implemented widely in vocational education and training.

It is interesting that schools are not always waiting for educational policymakers. In many schools teachers were already recognizing the potential and the relevance of IT in the very early stages of the development. Long before national, regional, and/or local policies were stimulating schools, many teachers took the initiative to get their schools involved in these new developments. The CompEd data show (Janssen Reinen & Plomp, 1993a) that in schools that are "early starters" in most cases teachers were the initiators to introduce computers in education, whereas "late starters" needed more external stimulation coming from external policies and/or the environment of the school (such as parents, business, and industry). The studies reported in this book illustrate that already in an early stage of the development the rich potential of IT for education was recognized in education. One can conclude that in many countries both policymakers and schools (often in the reversed order) have answered the "why" question positively. However, regardless of how positive policymakers and school administrators were in responding to the challenges of the ITs in our societies, we have to realize that this "rhetoric" can be implemented in various ways in educational practice; schools can vary largely in their activities with and applications of computers. Therefore, the "how" of implementing IT in the schools can be seen as indicative of the seriousness with which policymakers, school (district) boards and administrators have taken up the challenges of information age. Data about the actual use of computers will help us to find an answer to this question and, which may be even more important, to find recommendations for a better use of IT/computers in education.

In this context, it is relevant to distinguish between different ways IT (computers) can be used in education: as an "object," as an "aspect," and as a "medium" (Ministry of Education, 1992). In IT-as-object the focus is on the technical functioning of the technology, its social implications, and the possibility of employing particular applications in a useful way. Basically, this approach means teaching and learning about IT and computers; in lower secondary education often in introductory computer education or information and computer literacy courses, but also as part of existing subjects. IT-as-aspect refers to IT as an integrated component in another subject, such as in vocational courses or, in general education, in science courses. IT-as-a-medium refers to IT (or computers) as a tool or an aid in teaching and learning. Applications of IT as a medium are, for example, all forms of computer-assisted instruction. These different appearances of IT in education can be mapped globally on the policy rationales: the computer as an object can be considered as operationalization of the social rationale ("everybody needs to have some experience with computers"), IT-as-aspect realizes the vocational rationale, whereas IT-as-medium refers to the pedagogical rationale. Given the character of the studies reported here, most attention is spent on IT as object (or social rationale) and as medium (pedagogical rationale).

The results of many studies illustrate that the social rationale has been rooted broadly in education. It is generally accepted that IT, nowadays still predominantly computers, needs to be an integral part of the infrastructure of the schools and of children's experiences in school. The ITEC study illustrates for primary education how motivated children are in using computers in a variety of ways. In most countries, the use of the computer as object has been realized in lower secondary education by creating an introductory course in computer education, under such names as computer literacy, information literacy, or introductory computer science. The studies also make clear that students agree that computers are relevant and most of them enjoy using them.

Most schools in the countries reviewed in these studies are using computers also as a medium. The CompEd data reveal that most intensive use in elementary education in 1992 was playing games, learning new materials (tutorials) and drill and practice. In addition, some word processing is taking place. In lower secondary education most regular use of computers was also for learning new material, drill and practice, and word processing, while in 1992 in some countries there was still a great deal of programming (see Table 3.3).

How are these data about how computers are being used in schools helping us in getting a better understanding of the answer to the "why" question? Can we conclude, given the outcomes of CompEd and other studies, that in our schools the elaboration of the positive answers to the "why" question and its implementation is satisfactory? There is no unambiguous answer to these questions. If the goals of introducing computers in education would be to familiarize our students with IT (that is the social rationale), then we can be satisfied for the industrialized countries. (Almost) all students are working with computers during their school career, if not yet in primary school, then at least in lower secondary schools where a large majority of schools are teaching an introductory course in the use of computers. This can be considered a major accomplishment of our educational systems, of the schools, and especially of the teachers who have brought about this change in education.

We have to be more nuanced in our conclusions about the implementation of the use of IT-as-medium, the pedagogical rationale. The present usage of IT, predominantly of computers, can be characterized as that only a relatively small number of teachers are using computers for instructional purposes, and that the types of use are not very advanced, not using the full potential of the new technologies. Plomp and Voogt (1995) concluded that this situation reflects an implementation process in an early stage of development. They referred to Walker (1986), who stated that the easiest way for schools to respond to the challenge to "join the computer revolution" is to start with the easiest applications such as drill and practice and activities that involve taking the whole class to a computer laboratory. Walker pointed out that "anything else requires more money, more effort and expertise from teachers, and more variance from existing school practices" (p. 35). Plomp and Voogt (1995) stated that we should not be disappointed by this situation, particularly if one regards the use of computers in education as a complex innovation. With another reference to Walker: "If even a small part of the visionary dreams of computer-based education is to be realized, major changes will be required in the day-to-day activity and interaction patterns in classrooms. ... Developing these new patterns will require collaborative effort on a large scale sustained over a decade or more" (p. 33). They concluded from this that, the present situation with respect to computer use in education can be considered as the beginning stage of a process that could last many years. Given modern thinking about the broad goals of education, it is desirable that the use of IT in education develops further, away from the easiest responses to the technological challenges. Modern thinking about education is emphasizing the development of problem-solving skills, that students have to learn to construct their own knowledge, and be learning to learn. Typical for these approaches is that they are student-centered; they have an active role for students, who are challenged to make their reasoning explicit—and they confront students with the consequences of their reasoning. Such approaches are asking for new roles of teachers as they presuppose individualization of instruction. Instead of presenting scientific facts and theories to be learned, teachers have to become facilitators of the learning process and organizers of effective collaboration among students. Information technologies provide powerful applications that can be used to enhance the curriculum and the teaching/learning processes in these directions. For example, by using simulations students can gain an understanding of the reality by manipulation of critical variables. By working with modeling systems students gain an understanding of relations within a system. By working with microcomputer-based laboratories they can practice analyzing and interpreting data, and by retrieving and analyzing data from databases students can practice problem-solving skills. The CompEd data show that applications of this type are hardly occurring; some of them only exist in special project schools. Yet, in the future this type of application can be expected to be in line with current thinking about what goals should be accomplished in education. In conclusion, if the "why" question of IT is answered with the pedagogical rationale, that the use of computers as a medium can improve and enhance the teaching and learning processes, then our conclusion has to be that educational practice shows that we are only at the first phase of an implementation process.

What would be a good strategy to proceed from the stage where we are? Here, the recommendations of Fullan, Miles, and Anderson (1988) are appropriate. They suggest a process planning or adaptive approach in which a variety of strategic initiatives can be launched and in which there is a strong emphasis on learning from practical experience. They believe that the most promising strategies should center around developing the competence of teachers, training consultants, diffusing and supporting effective practices, networking, and building organizational capacity.

* * *

REFERENCES

Bower, C. A. (1988). *The cultural dimensions of educational computing*. New York: Columbia Teachers College Press.

Brown, A. (1994). The advancement of learning. *Educational Researcher, 23*(8), 4–12.

Christensen, R., Clayton, G., Campbell, N., & Knezek, G. (1994). *Water: A curriculum and technology infusion guide*. Denton: Texas Center for Educational Technology.

Collis, B. A. (Ed.). (1993). *The ITEC Project: Information Technology in Education and Children* (Final Report of Phase 1; ED/93/WS/17). Paris: UNESCO, Division of Higher Education.

Cuban, L. (1986). *Teachers and machines: The classroom use of technology since 1920*. New York: Teachers College Press.

Dobrin-Fujiki, M., Finau, S., & Knezek, G. (1995). A sustainable model for information technology training in Pacific Islands. *Proceedings of the Sixth World Conference on Computers in Education*. Birmingham, UK: Chapman & Hall.

Fullan, M.D., Miles, M.B., & Anderson, S.A.A. (1988). *A conceptual plan for implementing the new information technology in Ontario schools*. Ontario, Canada: Ministry of Education.

Hawkridge, D. (1991). Machine-mediated learning in third-world schools? *Machine-Mediated Learning, 3*, 319–328.

Janssen Reinen, I. A. M., & Plomp, Tj. (1993a). The decision phase: Starting to use computers. In W.J. Pelgrum & Tj. Plomp (Eds.), *The IEA study of computers in education: implementation of an innovation in 21 education systems*. Oxford, UK: Pergamon Press.

Janssen Reinen, I. A. M., & Plomp, Tj. (1993b). Gender and computers: Another area of inequity in education? In W. J. Pelgrum, I. A. M. Janssen Reinen, & Tj. Plomp (Eds.), *Schools, teachers, students and computers: A cross-national perspective*. Enschede, Netherlands: University of Twente Center for Applied Educational Research.

King, J. A. (1994–1995). Fear or frustration? Students' attitudes toward computers and school. *Journal of Research on Computing in Education, 27*(2), 154–170.

Knezek, G., & Miyashita, K. (1994). A preliminary study of the Computer Attitude Questionnaire. In G. Knezek (Ed.), *Studies on children and computers: The 1993–94 Fulbright series* (pp. 125–148). Denton: Texas Center for Educational Technology.

Knezek, G., Miyashita, K., & Sakamoto, T. (1990). Computers in education: Japan vs. the United States. In A. McDougall & C. Dowling (Eds.), *Computers in education* (pp. 775–780). North-Holland: Elsevier Science.

Knezek, G., Sakamoto, T., Yun, S. -Q., Ling, T., Loipha, S., & Cheamnakarin, P. (1994). Teacher training for information technology in four nations. In J. Willis, B. Robin, & D. A. Willis (Eds.), *Technology in teacher education annual, 1994* (pp. 14–17). New York: Allyn Bacon.

Knezek, G., Southworth, J., Christensen, R., Jones, G., & Moore, D. (1995). Educating teachers for hands-on science. In D. A. Willis, B. Robin, & J. Willis (Eds.), *Technology in teacher education annual, 1995* (pp. 186–190). New York: Allyn Bacon.

Krendl K. A., & Broihier, M. (1992).Student responses to computers: A longitudinal study. *Journal of Educational Computing Research, 8*(2), 215–227.

Kulik, C. -L. C., & Kulik, J. A. (1991). Effectiveness of computer-based instruction: An updated analysis. *Computers in Human Behavior, 7,* 75–94.

Kulik, J. A. (1994). Meta-analytic studies of findings on computer-based instruction. In E.L. Baker, & H.F., Jr. O'Neil (Eds.), *Technology assessment in education and training.* Hillsdale, NJ: Lawrence Erlbaum Associates.

Lai, K. W. (1993). Teachers as facilitators in a computer-supported learning environment. *Journal of Information Technology for Teacher Education, 2*(2), 127–137.

Lazarova, L. (1993, June). *Changes in children's creativity in Logo-based environment.* Paper presented to the IFIP Open Conference "Informatics and Changes in Learning," Gmunden, Austria.

Loipha, S., & Knezek, G. (1992, October). *Teachers' perceptions of computer use in elementary and secondary classrooms in Thailand* (With comparisons to the USA and Japan). Paper presented to the International Conference on Preparing Teachers for All the World's Children, Bangkok.

Ministry of Education and Sciences. (1992). *Enter: The future.* The Netherlands: Zoetermeer.

Murray-Lasso, M. A. (1993). Culture as a context and determinant of educational uses of information technology. In B. A. Collis (Ed.), *The ITEC Project: Information Technology in Education and Children* (Final Report of Phase 1; ED/93/WS/17). Paris: UNESCO, Division of Higher Education.

Nelson, C. S., & Watson, J. A. (1994). The computer gender gap: Children's attitudes, performance and socialization. In D. H. Wishnietsky (Ed.), *Assessing the role of technology in education* . Bloomington, IN: Phi Delta Kappa. (Reprinted from *Journal of Educational Technology Systems, 19*(4) pp. 345–353.)

Pelgrum, W. J., Janssen Reinen, I. A. M., & Plomp, Tj. (1993). *Schools, teachers, students and computers: A cross-national perspective.* The Hague: the International Association for the Evaluation of Educational Achievement.

Plomp, Tj., & Voogt, J. (1995). Use of computers. In B. J. Fraser & H. J. Walberg (Eds.), *Improving science education.* (pp. 171–185). Chicago: NSSE, The University of Chicago Press.

Rubstov, V. (1990, July 23). *Communicative-oriented learning technologies based on the use of computer nets.* Paper presented to the 22nd International Congress of Applied Psychology, Kyoto, Japan.

Sakamoto, A., & Sakamoto, T. (1993). Causal relationships between computer use, creativity, and motivation for learning in children: A panel survey of male elementary school students. *Educational Technology Research* (Japan), 16, 1–10.

Sheingold, D., & Hadley, M. (1990). *Accomplished teachers: Integrating computers into classroom practice.* New York: Bank Street College of Education.

Tzoneva, V., & Collis, B. [Moderators]. (1992, June 17). *ITEC Project: Technology and higher-level cognitive functions.* Invited panel presentation to the U.S. National Educational Computing Conference, Dallas, Texas.

Young, D. B., Gullickson-Morfitt, M., & Southworth, J. S. (1993). The HI-NEST Model: An international computer network for support of program implementation. *Pacific Telecommunications Conference Proceedings, 15,* 961–968.

Walker, D. F. (1986). Computers and the curriculum. In J. A. Culbertson & L. L. Cunningham (Eds.). *Microcomputers and education* (pp. 22–39). Chicago: NSSE, The University of Chicago Press.

Watson, D. (1993). *The Impact Report: An evaluation of the impact of information technology on children's achievements in primary and secondary schools.* London: Department of Education.

Wilder, G., Mackie, D., & Cooper, J. (1985). Gender and computers: Two surveys of computer-related attitudes. *Sex Roles, 13*(3/4), 215–228.

Appendix: Culture as a Context and Determinant of Educational Uses of Information Technology*

M. A. Murray-Lasso, Mexico

INTRODUCTION

Any activity in which humans participate is embedded in culture. Not to consider it distorts the facts in any study. On the other hand, culture is such a complicated concept that to take it into account requires the highest pattern recognition abilities of the human mind. Hence, any statement made about it can only be tentative and heavily tainted with the points of view of the researcher in question. The previous statements do not, or course, mean that nothing can be said about it. Even such subjective things as beauty can be talked about and many people will agree about them as long as they have some things in common (cultural traits.)

Culture is preserved in a group, tribe, or nation through education, whether formal or informal. When we try to introduce information technology (IT) into education one of the first things we run into is culture. Because most of the modern IT that we are interested in discussing here had its origin in English-speaking countries, in particular in the United States and the United Kingdom, much of it is tainted with that culture. To give a simple but important example, symbols used by the microcomputers used in education are coded in American Standard Code for Information Interchange (ASCII). Being an American (i.e., from the United States of America) code, it is completely oriented to the English language and no consideration was given to the possibility of writing in other languages, even those very close to English such as German or French. There is no possibility of using diacritical signs such as accents, or letters that do not appear in English.

*From: Collis, B. A. (Ed.). (1993). The ITEC PROJECT: Information Technology in Education and Children (Final Report of Phase 1; ED/93/WS/17; pp. 5.3-23–5.3-28). Paris: UNESCO, Division of Higher Education.

131

The extended ASCII code that is used by the IBM personal computers attempts to ameliorate this situation and with its 256 symbol code introduces many special symbols used in other West European languages, but it cannot be used in Greece or Russia where they use a completely different alphabet, not to speak of Japan or China for which it is more appropriate to speak of ideograms, given the very large number of symbols used. Even in countries, such as Israel, that do have an alphabet, a considerable amount of trouble arises from the fact that computers are designed to write from left to right while Hebrew is written from right to left.

The previous discussion gives a vivid indication that technology is not neutral as many claim but like any human endeavor is full of the culture of those that created it. Introducing IT to groups of people whose culture differs from that of the originators of the technology is bound to encounter all sorts of difficulties that may not have been obvious at first. In this appendix, I discuss some of the difficulties.

THE LANGUAGE QUESTION

Being one of the principal ingredients of culture, language stands out as one of the first things to consider when analyzing culture as context and determinant of educational uses of IT. Not only is there the difficulty of writing with a computer using the proper symbols in the different languages, a problem that has been quite successfully solved for many of the popular languages of the world, but not so for languages spoken by some other few millions of people; we are now thinking of the dominance of the English language in all things that have to do with computers: error comments, commands, manuals, books, magazines and journals, databases, network protocols, and so forth. In many countries the dominance is so apparent that knowing English is a generally accepted part of so called "computer literacy." So many words such as hardware and software, ROM, bug, CGA, debug, have been used untranslated in other languages for so many years that language academies that had attempted to introduce translations are giving up on them after a long fight. Even though many packages eventually get translated together with their documentation into other languages, because of the size of the markets of the English-speaking countries, the packages are originally developed for them.

Thus, by the time a package gets translated the original programs are already in their second or third versions. Therefore, we can see some countries in which popular packages such as dBASE that are being marketed for the IBM 1130 computer are still in the bookstore stands and are used by some teachers of computer programming who may or may not be aware of the number of years that such a machine has not been manufactured. People who want to be up to date (relatively speaking) have to do all their work directly in English, that is, using software in English; using manuals in English; using English keyboards; reading books, magazines and journals in English; and looking at videotapes in English. It is not only the undeveloped countries that are dominated by the English language. Industrially advanced countries such as Japan have to work in English as much as Paraguay or Morocco.

Some relief is provided by graphic-oriented protocols such as those introduced by the Macintosh machines that use a mouse, buttons, and icons. These are considerably more culturally transparent than English commands but not completely since they assume that the user belongs to the "computer culture." It is not at all obvious to a noncomputer-literate teacher what to do when faced with a screen full of icons (that may or may not mean anything to the teacher) enclosed in a frame that has several arrows pointing in different directions inside shaded rectangles in which a slightly smaller rectangle is outlined. You and I may know that by rolling the mouse until an arrow is inside the inscribed rectangle, pressing the right-hand-side button and holding it, while we roll the mouse in such a way that the rectangle moves together with the arrow button, and by holding it while we roll the mouse in such a way that the rectangle moves together with the arrow downwards, we can move to a window in a virtual page which has more icons to choose from. We also know that the relative size of the enclosing shaded rectangle has to do with the relative sizes of what is visible in the screen and what is available in the virtual page. But a noncomputer-literate teacher does not know it until it has been explained and demonstrated to him or her. That is the extent to which culture enters into communication with the computer whether graphic, written or oral.

THE COLONIZATION QUESTION

Many governments are concerned about the ever growing cultural colonization of poor countries by the English-speaking countries. It is not only in the field of computers that such a colonization is very apparent. The colonization is very strong in music, science, engineering, television, news and trade magazines, movies, scientific and technical books, videos, medicine, all sorts of machinery including automobiles, trucks, and airplanes and all the manuals that go with them, scientific journals and many other things including soft drinks and junk food. Educational software is just another step in this colonization process, but a very important step because it goes very deeply into the young minds of the children which are blank sheets of paper.

Systems of values different from the traditional one in a country can be transmitted very effectively through educational software (as was seen in early text books) in a manner that is inconspicuous. The competitive attitude of capitalism and free market economics, as opposed to a collaborative attitude of some cultures where religion is all important, for example, are imbedded in the competitive games with heavy emphasis on scores that are developed in industrialized countries. The fear of some governments of this cultural colonization is such that lacking educational software developed for and by members of their culture, they prefer to wait until this software is available rather than using foreign software in their public schools. Here is a clear example of how culture may determine the use of IT in education.

CURRICULUM DIFFERENCES, DIFFERENCES
IN STYLES OF TEACHING, SOCIAL ORGANIZATION,
AND NATIONAL IDENTITY

Different cultures approach the teaching question in different ways. Americans, for example, despite their "factory model" of education ("Vision: Test," 1990) have professed for many years a philosophy of education in which the students are welcome to search facts for themselves, question authority, look at things from different angles, and so forth. They believe that technology can help them make their educational system come closer to their educational philosophy. Not necessarily so with other cultures where power instead of coming from the people by democratic will comes from God or some other source. Given the role that Americans give to God and freedom of religion in their internal and foreign policy they would have to admit that authority coming from God is just as respectable as that coming from the people.

Despite this, they insisted after World War II that the emperor of Japan publicly renounce any divine origin that previous to the war was a central item in their social organization. Westerners have considerable difficulty understanding the importance that Arabs give to the Islamic Religion both in their everyday life and in matters of international relations. In countries where the authority comes from God, it has to eventually filter down to the government, teachers and parents. In such cultures truth is not a matter of independent research or a result of voting.

Thus, something is true because it was revealed by God through His representative on earth, which in the classroom are the teachers. Educational software of the kind in which a student discovers truth for himself is not well looked upon by such cultures. What is well looked upon is the tutorial type of software that first presents facts not open to question and then drills the students on those facts, there being only right and wrong answers. Naturally, it is difficult to find cultures in which the described situation is as pure as presented here, on either side. The actual facts are that different cultures have intermediate attitudes toward this matter. But the degree of authoritarianism has a lot to do with the type of educational software that may be acceptable in a given culture. In many countries educational adventure games such as the Carmen Sandiego software, even if translated and adapted culturally, would not be considered educational, but rather as play, because the custom is to stick to the national official curriculum so closely that even the homework for the day is published nationally in official newspapers, leaving the teachers almost no latitude to choose the manner in which to cover a topic.

In the developed nations many of the topics that are included in their curricula have been covered in various degrees by educational software developed within their culture. However, in undeveloped countries, many of the topics that are included in their curricula have not been covered either by them or by software developers in industrialized countries. Such is the case with topics having to do with local history, local forms of government, local literature, and other topics not of general interest (such as mathematics) but of little interest except to the country in question. The reasons why these topics have not been covered by educational software generally have to do with economics. The most prevalent is a lack of an interesting profitable market. The economic situation of many of these countries is that the schools have no electricity, no budgets to buy even paper, books or chalk, thus installing computers is out of the question except possibly in some of the private schools which generally are a small minority.

In many of these countries the private schools are run by foreign communities that can get educational software from their countries of origin in the language of that country. Because in almost all instances the schools are bilingual, there is a perfect excuse to use software in the other language as part of the bilinguality. However, this software is usually designed to cover the curricula of the country of origin and thus does not cover topics in the curricula mentioned above. This, of course, tends to increase the cultural colonialism of industrial countries. We thus find that in these bilingual schools, just to give an example, political leaders of the mother country may be better known by the students, particularly in what they have done and what they stand for, than local political leaders, among other reasons because the educational materials (not only those computer based) in the culture of the mother country are much better than the local ones.

This together with the monopoly of the communications industry, particularly television from the advanced countries, creates a situation that many governments find very undesirable; loss of national identity. This fear is reflected in a rejection of the use of computers and other foreign technologies such as videotapes in education both for private and public schools.

POLITICAL, ECONOMIC, AND TRADE CONSIDERATIONS

To provide each student in a country with a computer is something that even advanced countries have found too expensive to do. Average national ratios now stand at something between 20 to 30 students per computer in countries like the United States with interested groups recommending that by 1995 the ratios become five students per computer. In a country where computers are manufactured and there is a strong software development community the installation of many computers in the educational system benefits both the students and the local industry; it creates jobs and improves the economy.

Such benefits are not so clear in the case of countries where most or all the computers have to be imported using hard currency. The benefits to the students have to be so clear that seldom is the evidence strong enough to really convince the politicians that allocate the budgets. Additionally, some countries have imposed trade restrictions on the export of certain technical equipment that may have military applications such as computers. Such was the case of the United States and Cuba and until very recently with the former Communist Block.

Seen from the undeveloped countries' point of view, bringing in equipment that they do not have the technology to manufacture in order to help operate crucial national systems creates a dependency of the undeveloped countries on the suppliers that is politically very undesirable because it weakens the national sovereignty. There have been several instances where national governments forbade their national companies from supplying countries that they are pressuring politically or economically, creating a very difficult situation in the undeveloped country. Although the educational system is not generally considered as a particularly vulnerable system in a country when compared with the financial, communications or food supply system, IT has acquired the reputation of being one of the technologies that countries may use to pressure other countries with good leverage because of the dependency from it of such activities as banking, communications, and transportation. Therefore, there are governments that are somewhat reluctant to have their educational system depend too much on computers and other equipment that are in the hands of foreign companies and that are not manufactured locally.

Local politics rather than international politics may also enter into the picture. The microcomputer has given rise to, among other things, desktop publishing. Many regimes base their control of the population on the fact that they control the news and the communication systems and they do not look favorably on any breach of their monopoly on such items. In such countries a person having a mimeograph machine, a radio transmitter or a VCR is suspected of being reactionary and becomes a candidate for close surveillance and even imprisonment. Such countries are unlikely to be in favor of giving teachers personal computers for educational purposes, since they suspect the machines may be used for subversive activities. They will find all sorts of reasons to avoid the real introduction of computers in education. They may give lip service to the idea for international image purposes but more likely than not the introduction will be slowed down to a trickle and will flow only to the most politically trustworthy groups. Often a good excuse is the economic woes of the country, in spite of the fact that enormous sums of money are spent for political propaganda and personal image building by dictators.

CONCLUSIONS

The cultural aspect of introducing IT in education is a very vast and complicated topic. A very short and incomplete discussion has been given with the limited goal of inviting the reader to reflect on the topic. The question of how to characterize culture by the measurement of specific variables is left completely untouched. We believe the indicators used by international organizations are not sufficiently precise to base useful models for research on them. These indicators say nothing of how authoritarian a regime is, what is the degree of colonization of a country by others, what is the degree of national identity in a country, and other items mentioned in the article as important in the analysis of the use of computers in education. It is this researcher's position that this question of the role of culture in the use of computers in education has to be handled for the time being in as anecdotal manner as possible, as many things are involved in a complicated process such as education. Statistical indices such as the number of students per computer in a country are of very little significance if culture is not taken into consideration.

I believe this is true even when speaking of states within the same country. Thus, the educational benefits of introducing computers in urban Washington, DC would be very different from the ones that could be reaped in North Dakota because of the cultural environment. Facts such as living in a rural area with not that many social things to do because the next door neighbor lives 15 miles away, versus living in a ghetto area where peer pressure may be an overwhelming factor in the behavior of a young person (who may be lured into drugs because it is the thing to do if one is really a macho man) can completely annul the significance of an indicator such as students/computers.

The conclusion of this appendix is that it is urgent to do more research on the cultural aspects of the use of computers in education. The thesis is also that for the present we do not have good indicators to measure the cultural aspects that seem to really matter and that counting the number of libraries per 1,000 inhabitants is not nearly sufficient to build statistical models that make any sense in questions such as the subject of this appendix. We will for some time have to do qualitative analysis of these matters rather than statistical quantitative analysis. This should not discourage us since we know that education and culture are extremely complex topics and we should not have expected them to yield with the same ease that some industrial problems have to mathematics and statistics.

REFERENCES

Collis, B. A. (Ed.). (1993). *The ITEC Project: Information Technology in Education and Children* (Final Report of Phase 1; ED/93/WS/17). Paris: UNESCO, Division of Higher Education.

Vision: Test (Technologically Enriched Schools of Tomorrow), Final Report, Recommendations for American Educational Decision Makers. (1990). Eugene, OR: ISTE.

About the Authors

Betty A. Collis, Faculty of Educational Science and Technology, University of Twente, The Netherlands. Dr. Collis is an associate professor of educational instrumentation. She was co-principal investigator, along with Dr. Assen Jablensky of the National Neuropsychology Research Programme in Bulgaria, of the ITEC Project, one of the studies featured in this book, and is currently involved in two European and two national projects involving the use of telecommunications in education. She is past president of the International Council for Computers in Education (now the International Society for Technology in Education) and is currently chairperson of the Working Group on Research in Informatics in Education for the International Federation of Information Processing, Technical Committee 3. She received her bachelor's degree in mathematics from the University of Michigan, her master's in mathematics education from Stanford University, and her doctorate in measurement and evaluation of computer applications in education from the University of Victoria, Canada.

* * *

Gerald A. Knezek, University of North Texas, Denton, Texas. Dr. Knezek is associate professor of technology and cognition and currently holds the Matthews Chair for Research in Education at the University of North Texas. Along with Miyashita and Sakamoto, he served as co-principal investigator for the Young Children's Computer Inventory Project that, during 1990 to 1993, assessed the psychological impact of computer use on primary school children in three nations. He was a Fulbright Scholar at the Tokyo Institute of Technology and Japan's National Center for University Entrance Examinations from 1993 to 1994. He received his AB in mathematics and the social sciences from Dartmouth College, and his master's in education and doctorate degrees in educational psychology from the University of Hawaii.

* * *

Kwok-Wing Lai, University of Otago, New Zealand. Dr. Lai is a senior lecturer at the Department of Education, University of Otago, New Zealand. He did his postgraduate studies in educational technology and computer applications in education at Queen's University and the Ontario Institute for Studies in Education (OISE), Canada. He is the editor of *Computers in New Zealand Schools* and his current research focuses on the uses of computer-mediated communication in the school curriculum.

* * *

Keiko T. Miyashita, Tokyo Institute of Technology, Japan. Dr. Miyashita was a Japan Society for the Promotion of Science postdoctoral fellow at the Tokyo Institute of Technology when work began on this book. She served as co-principal investigator, along with Dr. Knezek and Dr. Sakamoto, on the Young Children's Computer Inventory Project. She received her bachelor's degree in education from Aoyama Gakuin University, Tokyo, and her master's and doctorate degrees in early childhood education from the University of North Texas.

* * *

Willem J. Pelgrum, University of Twente, Center for Applied Educational Research, The Netherlands. Dr. Pelgrum is coordinator of research in the Center for Applied Educational Research at the University of Twente, the Netherlands. His main professional activities are in the area of international comparative research. He was the national research coordinator in the Netherlands of international assessments in mathematics and science. He is the international coordinator of the IEA Computers in Education study. He is currently also involved in conducting a training program for educational researchers from 10 countries in Central and Eastern Europe.

* * *

Tjeerd Plomp, Faculty of Educational Science and Technology, University of Twente, Enschede, the Netherlands. Dr. Plomp is professor of education with a focus on curriculum and educational technology. Together with Dr. Pelgrum, he was responsible for the international comparative survey of computers in education, which was conducted under the auspices of IEA, the International Association for the Evaluation of Educational Achievement. He is since 1990 chair of IEA. He also served during the 1980s as advisor to the Dutch government for the area of information technology in education. He received his master's degree in mathematics, and his doctorate in social sciences, both from Free University, Amsterdam.

* * *

Takashi Sakamoto, National Institute of Multimedia Education, Japan. Dr. Sakamoto is director-general of the National Institute of Multimedia Education and professor emeritus at the Tokyo Institute of Technology. He served as co-principal investigator, with Dr. Knezek and Dr. Miyashita, for the Young Children's Computer Inventory Project; as a member of researchers in ITEC with Dr. Collis and Dr. Lai; and also worked as a local member of the IEA project in Japan. He received his bachelor's, master's, and doctorate degress in psychology from the University of Tokyo. He is president of the Japan Society of Educational Technology and a member of the Science Council of Japan. He is also a member of the Central Commission of Education and the National Council of Educational Personnel Training.

Author Index

Numbers in *italics* indicate pages with complete bibliographic information.

Subject Index

For Product Safety Concerns and Information please contact our EU representative GPSR@taylorandfrancis.com Taylor & Francis Verlag GmbH, Kaufingerstraße 24, 80331 München, Germany

T - #0027 - 270225 - C0 - 229/152/9 [11] - CB - 9780805820737 - Gloss Lamination